Annia Regilla
Her Cenotaph
A Tale of Two Cultures

ANNIA REGILLA
HER CENOTAPH
A TALE OF TWO CULTURES

John Graham

For Ophelia, with special thanks for the music!
From John

MELISENDE

© John Graham 2016

The right of John Graham to be identified as the author of this work has been asserted by him in accordance with the Copyright, Designs and Patents Act 1988.

All rights reserved. No part of this work, its text or any or part of the illustrations and drawings, may be reproduced, stored in a retrieval system, or transmitted in any form or by any means, electronic, mechanical, photocopying, recording or otherwise, without the prior permission of the copyright owner.

Annia Regilla
Her Cenotaph
A Tale of Two Cultures

First published 2016 by
Melisende, London
ISBN 9781901764 72 7

www.melisende.com

All photographic material is copyright the author unless otherwise indicated.

Printed and bound in England by 4edge

To Britt

my partner in what follows

CONTENTS

	Acknowledgements	IX
	Prologue	1
I	The Rome Scholarship	3
II	Driving to Rome	9
III	The British School at Rome	13
IV	A Roman rediscovery	15
V	Life at the British School	21
VI	Christmas in Vienna	25
VII	Annia Regilla grows up	27
VIII	Herodes Atticus, multi-millionaire	31
IX	The Roman necropolis beneath St Peter's	33
X	Engagement in Venice	37
XI	In Rome and the Campagna	43
XII	Annia and Herodes' early married years	47
XIII	To Sicily in search of Vikings	49
XIV	In Sicily	55
XV	Annia and Herodes move to Athens	61
XVI	Annia as Priestess	65
XVII	Herodes on trial	71
XVIII	Herodes' tributes to Annia	75
XIX	The Cenotaph	81
XX	Return from Rome. Marriage in Sweden.	89

XXI	Life in the New Town	95
XXII	Key buildings in Harlow and new horizons	103
XXIII	The Harvey Centre completes the plan	113
XXIV	Working with Frederick Gibberd	117
XXV	A new career	125
XXVI	We buy a Swedish house and travel	131
XXVII	Harlow languishes. Gibberd Gallery obtained.	139
	Epilogue	143
	Appendix	148
	List of Illustrations	157
	Bibliography	160

ACKNOWLEDGEMENTS

Many people have helped with the development of this story since I first encountered the Cenotaph building over sixty years ago. To all of them I owe thanks; they are characters in the text.

Since beginning work on the book friends Judith Misins, Sue Powell and David Beazley helped with items of early research and Suzanne Eustace typed the first part of my handwritten script. The interest from friends in England has been continuous and the British School at Rome has been encouraging since hearing about the project.

From my relatives and friends in Sweden I have been spurred on by their eager interest and I have received helpful expert advice from my nephew, Peter Bäckström, who is a Librettist, theatre director and associate professor of music and drama at the Royal Danish Academy of Music in Copenhagen.

For publisher, my first choice would have been Longman with whose headquarters offices in Harlow I had been intimately involved, but sadly this building was demolished following the takeover of the firm by another organisation. When I decided to self-publish, therefore, I was surprised and delighted to find that the director of the local firm I approached had in fact been part of Longman for twelve years. The experience of working with Alan Ball of Melisende and its editor Leonard Harrow has been a pure pleasure and very much the 'hands on' experience I would have wished.

For the cover design I have called upon another local firm, Menor, whose director, Nigel Moore, was responsible for recreating from the negatives which survived my lost measured drawing of the building which is the central pivot of the book.

Finally, my special thanks are for Sue McDonald, my personal assistant, who completed the typing of my manuscript, photographed my paintings and drawings and made it all digital. Then, together with Alan, Len and Nigel we worked to produce a book which we hoped would be a pleasure to read and also to handle, and would be worthy of its title.

John Graham
March 2016

PROLOGUE

When the richest man in the second century AD Graeco-Roman world builds a memorial to his wife, who has died suddenly in controversial circumstances, it is likely to be something special.

Athenian Herodes Atticus inherited his riches from the discovery of buried treasure near the Acropolis. His wife Annia Regilla came from a rich Roman aristocratic family. Their marriage, like mine, was a union of two cultures.

The building was of modest size and erected on their estate near the Via Appia in the Roman Campagna where they had enjoyed peace and beauty. Centuries passed and Rome experienced turbulent times. The building was robbed of its contents and marble elements were removed. A small farm grew up beside it and the building was used as an outhouse, stuffed with hay and frequented by chickens.

That is how I found it in the winter of 1953. My Italian guide book identified it as 'Tempio del Dio Redicolo'—a temple dedicated to the god who had persuaded Hannibal to turn in his tracks, and it was believed that a visit, on leaving Rome, ensured return.

At that time I did not know about Herodes and Annia, but I did recognise that even in its partly ruined state I had in front of me a building of rare and special beauty, and I decided to devote my time in Rome to measuring it.

How I came to be in Rome is a story which begins more than a year earlier …

1 *Professor R A Cordingley, Consultant Architect.*

When this building, which was completed in 1935, was featured in the Architectural Review *critic Julian Leathart wrote of it:*

'The extreme diversity in shape and site relationship of the component units comprising this scheme would appear to present an almost unsurmountable barrier to the achievement of homogeneity, which is so essential in good composition. Yet so skilfully have these units been welded together that there is no indication of untidiness arising from scattered loose ends. Every section is related in context and there is an intrinsic shapeliness of form and contour through the whole composition; moreover, the building groups well from diverse points of view in a most remarkable manner. The vigorous, sure handling of the mass and line, or surface relationship and of silhouette, have produced a sculpturesque quality of high order.

And concluded:

Collaboration between engineer and architect has rarely been carried to so felicitous a conclusion as at the Rising Sun Colliery; future industrial building may well gain in seemliness and precision by following this notable precept.

J.R. LEATHART.

As a fifteen year old, looking out for examples of modern architecture, I first saw Professor Cordingley's building illustrated when a perceptive grammar school history master gave me a small book Towards a New Britain *which had been published by the Architectural Press to accompany a wartime RIBA exhibition in London. Little did I know I would begin studying under Prof. Cordingley at Manchester University two years later.*

I
THE ROME SCHOLARSHIP

I looked down from one of the tall windows in the Henry Florence Hall onto Portland Place. In the early morning hours it was deserted and the facades opposite looked like stage sets. I was wondering if I had done enough on my design and should try to get a few hours' sleep on the camp bed which was behind me in one of the curtained cubicles temporarily created as workplaces for the ten Prix de Rome finalists.

We had arrived at the headquarters building of the Royal Institute of British Architects, been handed the design brief and ushered to our drawing boards. Lunch was taken together at a large table in the middle of the echoing hall presided over by the RIBA Secretary to see that our conversations stayed innocuous. Even our necessary visits to the toilets in the basement were accompanied.

The design brief, so far as I recall, was for a big scheme. I felt tired, and thought I could complete the drawing the next morning before the noon deadline. So I stretched out on my camp bed and became probably one of the very few people ever to sleep in the Henry Florence Hall.

Some weeks later I heard I had been selected for the last stage of the competition, which was to prepare full design drawings for a College of Art. This took most of the summer and I retreated to a back bedroom in my parents' house in Manchester where I would receive regular meals from loving hands and be able to concentrate.

I had already completed a five year-degree course in architecture at Manchester University and when I eventually heard that I had been placed first and would be going to Rome, it was to my professor, Reginald Cordingley, that I went for advice on what I should study there. 'Prof' was regarded with a mixture of affection and awe by his students. He himself had been awarded the Prix de Rome in 1923 and we had seen some of his immaculately beautiful measured drawings of Renaissance and Roman buildings. We knew that his life had contained tragedy; the loss of his young wife leaving him to bring up his son alone; and we also knew that he had designed one of

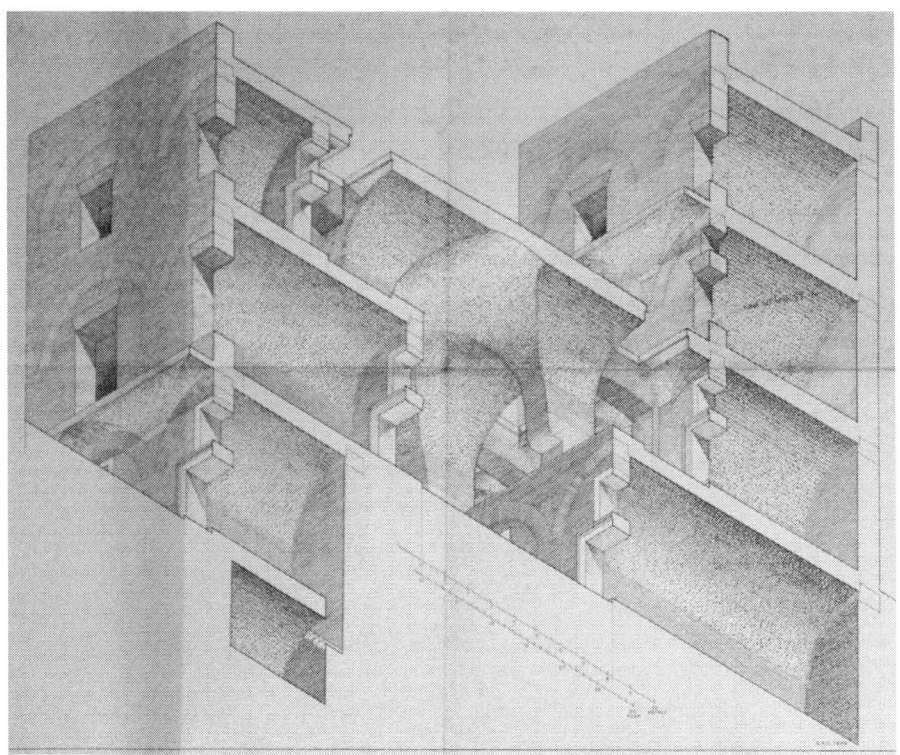

2a Professor Cordingley's axonometric drawing of the covered hall and multi-level shops of the Roman Markets of Trajan.
  b John Graham's cross-section drawing of the Markets of Trajan with dimensions

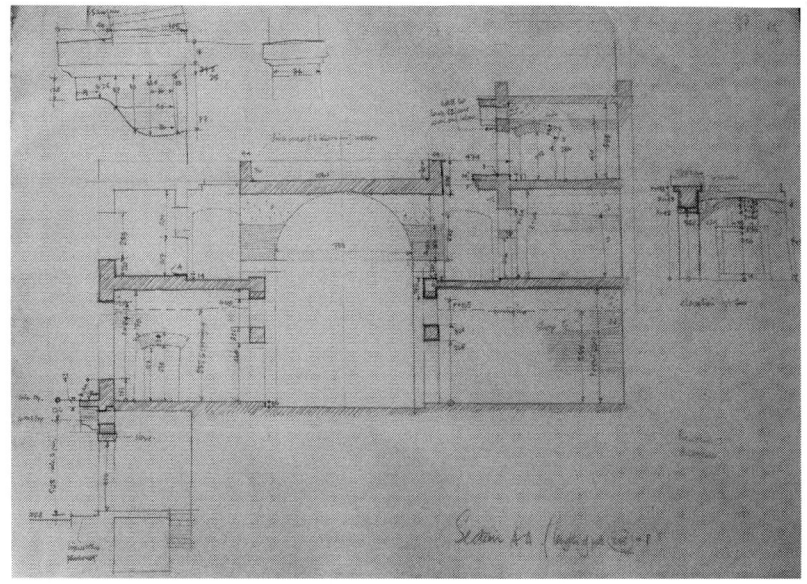

the earliest examples of purely functional modern architecture in England, and his small booklet *Everyday Architecture* was, and still is for me, the best definition of the subject. I was eager to listen.

After a general talk, he produced a print of an axonometric drawing he had done of the Markets of Trajan, a multi-level covered shopping complex which is the true ancestor of all present-day shopping malls, including the Harlow one I was to work on with Sir Frederick Gibberd some twenty-five years later.

'You could take some check dimensions for me', said Prof, 'and then there is a small building I saw which is a fascinating example of Roman decorative brickwork. I would like some photographs and measured information so that I can include it in the new edition of Bannister Fletcher which I am preparing. You will find it in the countryside and it is known as the Temple of Deus Rediculus.'

I returned to Harlow where I had been working for the Development Corporation for several months. Experience in the army of occupation in post-war Germany, and years among ruined cities had convinced me that the most worthwhile work for an architect was to be part of the creation of a new town, and a talk by a young Architect Planner, Frederick Gibberd, to an audience of Manchester architects and students about his Master Plan for Harlow had shown me the man I wanted to work with. So I answered the first advertisement I saw for a job in Harlow and got it. Considering I had only been working there for less than a year it was extremely generous of the Corporation to allow me leave of absence to take up the prize, but so they did, and in October 1953 I was ready to leave for Rome.

There was, however, a decision to be made. Three years previously, frustrated by slowness of cycling and the imprecision of hitch-hiking, I had invested £75 of my limited student finances in the purchase of a car. I had found a 1931 Morris 8 two-door convertible which, although twenty-years old and with an unspecified number of miles under its belt, appeared to be in sound condition. It was very basic. There were no synchromesh gears, but I had been taught the art of double de-clutching when taking driving lessons. There was no petrol pump. The gravity fed tank was above the four cylinder engine, in a perilous position I now realise. There was no starter motor, a handle was supplied and one learned to beware of the back kicks which could put a thumb out of joint. The canvas hood folded right back and the celluloid side windows just lifted out leaving a completely open tourer. There was only one windscreen wiper and the two side indicator arrows sometimes had to be assisted by well-placed blows before they came out of their boxes; but one could always give hand signals. More importantly, it was strong, with a steel chassis, and its bodywork could be easily repainted. Speed was unimportant to me, but it could reach 50 mph or more with a favourable tailwind; and I liked its looks. Used daily it responded well and I had already driven it for hundreds of miles the previous summer in Sweden. I could not abandon it. I must drive to Rome.

3a   1951 Festival of Britain.   Barbara Hepworth's Contrapuntal Forms and Transport pavilion.

3b   Visiting Gröndal low rental apartments by architects Bäckström and Keinius, Stockholm, 1952.

II
DRIVING TO ROME

Unlike Herodes, I did not have to travel to Rome to meet my wife-to-be. We had already met two summers previously in London. With my newly purchased car, I had decided to drive down to London from Manchester and spend the summer vacation at the 1951 Festival of Britain. This post-war celebration of art, architecture and design promised to be exciting and the first opportunity to experience a completely modern environment of buildings and sculpture. But much more awaited me.

When I called at a friend's house in Richmond where I hoped to stay I was met by a lovely blonde whose beautiful voice was slightly touched by the melody of a Swedish accent. She seemed an angel, as beautiful in spirit as appearance—an opinion I never had cause to change in the fifty-four years we were to be together—and we fell deeply in love.

That first summer passed in a whirl of delight, and when we parted in September I vowed to visit Sweden the next year, which I did, shipping the car as deck cargo from Manchester to Gothenburg where we met and then toured Sweden from Dalarna north of Stockholm to her family's farm in southern Skåne. Then again we had to part. I returned to England and soon found my position at Harlow, while Britt, who was studying singing at Malmö Conservatory and was already receiving glowing press notices for her concert appearances, would travel to Vienna for a second winter with Viennese teachers (see Appendix).

In that city there was a rich musical life with wonderful opera performances and on the side of a programme of *Der Rosenkavalier* dated 25 December 1952 Britt wrote; 'John I longed so much for you and to the time when we once again can be *together* to see and hear the things we love. I hope it won't be long, love lilla.'

In driving to Rome I would be moving closer to Britt in Vienna and the future seemed bright. It was, though, a difficult time of year for the journey. The days were short and often wet. My memories are more of glistening wet roads than sunlit landscapes. It was also the time of the sugar beet harvest in northern France and the roads were busy with trucks piled high and, somewhat precariously, with their loads which, once squashed, rendered themselves a slippery menace. My narrow tyres did not have a very good grip and I shall never forget the graphic road signs showing a skidding car above the word '*Betteraves*!'

Moreover, my little car had been modified sometime during its first twenty years by the removal of its headlights and their substitution by a single low-placed spotlamp. The French lorry drivers hated it, and once darkness came I was forced off the roads by their barrage of bright lights. So I spent long evenings in French cafés reading Frederick Gibberd's writings on the design of residential areas in a new Ministry of Housing publication, and eating a daily slice of rich fruit cake specially supplied by my grandparents' bakery. Whether it was the sustaining powers of such nourishment or my thoughts filled with love and a sense of adventure, but I was able to press on doggedly day after day.

Britt, in Vienna, received two postcards from me. The first was written from Vienne, about fifteen miles south of Lyon on the Thursday, and I was bemoaning a sore backside from all the bumps in the roads and the cobblestones *(pavé)* in the French towns, which were rarely by-passed in those days. I wrote: 'Fog and mist all day, as well, but the car is wonderful and the sun is getting stronger each day. On Saturday I'll be in Italy and Monday in Rome. It's not far now, but I don't want to travel so far alone again.' (I never had to). On Saturday I wrote from Genoa: 'Only two more days driving to do. Italy is much more lovely than France in every way. There is sun, flowers, beauty and kind people—and cheaper too.'

Then, when I was no more than twenty miles from Rome, and could almost see it on the horizon, and lest I should suffer from hubris about my achievement, the engine suddenly cut out.

It was late afternoon and there was a certain amount of traffic moving towards Rome so, as I had done many times before, I began to hitch. I soon got help but in an unusual form. It was a small three-wheeled motorcycle-powered van that stopped for me; one of those clever post-war contraptions designed for economy. It was, the driver told me, my car that interested him. I explained that I had checked it over and found nothing mechanically wrong but suspected an electrical fault. This later proved to be the case. Learning of my destination he offered to tow me there. And so it was that, at the end of a suitably long rope and in gathering darkness, I arrived at the British School, parked at the rear and went in to register my arrival while my helper, suitably rewarded, sped off.

4   The entrance façade of the British School at Rome. Sir Edwin Lutyens' adaptation of the upper order of the west front of St Pauls. (Photo courtesy of the British School at Rome)

III
THE BRITISH SCHOOL AT ROME

Arriving in the dark and, so to speak, at the tradesman's entrance to the British School I was not struck by the imposing Lutyens' facade or the great flight of south facing steps which fronts it. When I did come to size up my surroundings I found a rather unusual building which was the result of an unusual history.

The Prix de Rome had been initiated by the Académie de France in the seventeenth century and the German and French Schools were set up in the 1870s but it was not until 1901 that a British School was opened in a Roman palazzo with no residential accommodation for students. There it remained for fourteen years until, following the International Exhibition of 1911 in Rome, it was agreed that the site on the Pincian Hill occupied by the British pavilion would be granted in perpetuity to the British nation on condition that it was to be used only as a British School. The 1851 Commission in London which had inherited funds from the Great Exhibition of that year (a direct ancestor of the recent 1951 Festival of Britain) agreed to meet the costs of acquiring the pavilion and converting it. Sir Edwin Lutyens had designed the exhibition pavilion and the Board of Trade had given him the condition that for the facade he was to copy the upper order of the west front of St Paul's. His skilful adaptation had proved very popular.

The conversion of the rest of the pavilion, however, was beset with difficulties. From 1913 onwards the architect was concerned with a bigger job, the Viceroy's Palace in New Delhi, and made matters worse by insisting that the building work in Rome should be carried out by an English contractor and using many English components shipped out from England. The outbreak of war and the occasional sinking of supplies and the involvement of three committees, one in Rome and two in England, compounded the problems. When the school was eventually opened in 1916 it was scarcely two thirds finished and Lutyens' plans had been modified several times. In fact the Common Room/Dining Room with its imposing fireplace of Lutyens proportions was not finished until the end of 1924 and was designed by Harold Bradshaw, the first Rome Scholar in Architecture.

Apart from the original Lutyens Entrance Hall and this rather grand Dining Room the rest of the accommodation was extremely modest and grouped around a small central courtyard. I was given one of the seven artists' studios on the north side, high ceilinged and sparsely furnished, with a sleeping gallery at mezzanine level.

We were a small community of a dozen or so with the majority being artists. Since the 1920s the mixture of archaeologists, architects and artists had worked well and I found the atmosphere of freedom and stimulation delightful. The director was an archaeologist, John Ward Perkins, at that time in the eighth year of what would prove to be the longest directorship in the school's history—twenty-nine years. But we Rome Scholars were expected to be self-motivated and to work without direction. What we did was up to us.

Daily we met for meals in the grand Dining Hall served by white jacketed staff over whom presided Bruno Bonelli, who had joined the staff as a youth and had been in charge since 1926. Bruno was a firm character and would only speak to us or respond in Italian. I soon learnt that I could not get away with a nod if I wished to have a second helping of delicious gnocchi, for that was taken as a negative.

After exploration of the school's immediate surroundings and the correction of the electrical fault on the car, which I found to be a loose wire to a 'secret' safety switch a previous owner had fixed beneath the dashboard, I was ready to find the temple I had come so far to seek.

IV
A ROMAN REDISCOVERY

From the south facing front of the British School on the upper slopes of the Pincian Hill I drove down the curving roads and terraces of the Pincio gardens shaded by umbrella pines and cypresses to the Piazza del Populo below. Vespas buzzed by me. These neatly designed machines called for no special gear. You sat on them in everyday dress and your girlfriend sat side saddle behind you, her outstretched legs balancing your turns and her unhelmeted hair blowing in the breeze you created.

The Piazza del Populo was the finest entrance any city could have. It was here that the newly abdicated Queen Christina of Sweden entered through the Porta de Populo to take up residence in Rome, and an inscription composed by the Pope *Felici fausto ingressi* ('for a happy and blessed entrance') bearing the date 1655 commemorates the event. The second oldest obelisk in Rome punctuated the square at its centre and as I turned to enter Rome I was faced by the twin churches of S Maria di Monte Santo and S Maria dei Miracoli specially designed and built to mark the entrances to the three roads which fan out from them into the city.

I took the central one, Via del Corso, which led straight to the great iced cake of the Victor Emmanuel Monument and beyond it to great tiered oval of the Colosseum, where I turned right into the Via di S Gregorio making for the southern gate in the city wall, the Porta San Sebastiano, which led in turn onto the Via Appia Antica. The traffic was busy and the Italian drivers were quite competitive at the large intersections but they treated me with a certain respect and I suspect that they saw I had little to lose in the event of a scratch.

Once outside Rome I was in a different world. This was the Campagna which in Classical times had been an area of great natural beauty until it was devastated during the barbarian invasions and then blighted by malaria. It was now little visited. Wild flowers and grasses grew among the many tombs which punctuated the ancient road built by Appius Claudius in 312 BC where the original stones still remained for long stretches. The road led south straight as a die to the Alban Hills and in the direction of Naples. This was the way Paul had entered Rome.

5a-c John Graham's photographs of the building as first seen 'stuffed with hay and frequented by chickens'.

From the Via Appia my 1933 Italian touring guide gave directions off to a Via della Caffarella and then to a temple referred to as 'Tempio del Dio Redicolo'. The final approach was along farm roads but the car being narrow and light there were no problems. Then I saw my objective, an apparently square building of medium height with some lower farm buildings close to it, and I was amazed.

This was not a ruin as I had been accustomed to find among English abbeys half this age. Here there were no truncated shapes of lichen encrusted stone, but a beautifully proportioned little building faced with yellow ochre or russet coloured brick and richly decorated with capitals and entablatures of moulded or carved terracotta. In the thin winter sunshine the details appeared crisp, and on the side wall which faced me was an extraordinary feature. Dividing the wall into three sections were octagonal columns of russet brick set into semi-circular niches! It was a detail I had never seen before, or have since, and it was a perfect enrichment of the wall surface. I knew I had before me a small architectural masterpiece of some sophistication.

It was clearly being used by the neighbouring farm. Chickens ran in and out and it was stuffed with hay. Although a tiled roof appeared intact the whole front of the building had been removed together with the window surrounds and inscription panels. But there was clearly enough remaining to measure the building and the idea began to dawn on me that I should attempt a reconstruction of it in its original polychromatic beauty.

Measuring buildings or monuments and then producing drawings of them had formed part of my architectural education. I had measured fonts in Cheshire churches and together with a fellow student, Peter Liley, had measured the York Water Gate, now in gardens a little way back from the Thames. We had also been to Milan and measured the graceful early Renaissance portico by Bramante which fronted the church of Abbiategrasso. The portfolios of student work submitted by the university for initial entry to the Rome Scholarship would have contained such measured drawings, but in this electronic age it is no longer a requirement.

In 'stretching a line' upon a building one became aware of the thought process of the designer. This can be revealing.

I recalled how three of us were once measuring a wall pulpit in Chester Cathedral and were being frustrated by its inconsistencies. A Jabberwocky-like typing error in a letter from the Chapter Clerk; 'snet your drawings to The Chapter Chark', sparked off a jingle which contained the following lines:

> 'Twas Cheester and the architotes did tape and tumble in a tangle,
> All footly were the measured notes and did the plumly lines outdangle.
> 'Beware the Goth-Goth work my son, the mouldly arch; the angley wall … '

We had found few right angles and every arched opening varied in size. It was a nightmare.

This building, I trusted, would be different and despite its size I felt I could tackle it single handed. The people in the farm raised no objection to my proposed visits. A ladder was promised when needed and I set about making the sketch drawings on which I would record the measurements during the coming weeks. All I needed to do was keep at it and not get discouraged by the difficulties which would come.

6   *Landscape near Veii. Watercolour by John Graham.*
'in the cold penetrating winter light the countryside seemed empty …save for an isolated necropolis ….'

V
LIFE AT THE BRITISH SCHOOL

Life at the British School was very congenial. I especially liked being in the company of artists and found them rather different from the architects and academics I had previously known. Perhaps finding it difficult to explain what they were doing made them less sure of themselves and more sensitive to others? I made a mental note to know more artists in the future and this I eventually did decades later when I ran an art gallery in Harlow.

Here in Rome I particularly admired the powerful and well-structured drawings and paintings being produced by Derrick Greaves, and another painter, Heinz Inlander, in a more tentative style, seemed to have caught the spirit of the Italian landscape. I had first begun to attempt painting for its own sake, rather than as a useful illustration of an architectural design, four years previously on a visit to Ibiza in the days before it had been discovered by hippies and package tourists. So one day I took time off from measuring and drove out north of Rome in the direction of Veii where the pre-Roman Etruscans had lived.

In the cold penetrating winter light the countryside seemed empty and deeply asleep, save for an isolated necropolis surrounded by the motionless sentinels of dark cypresses. There was a feeling of timelessness, and in line and watercolour wash I tried to capture this, no doubt influenced by the work I was seeing at the School.

There was a sculptor, Sean Rice, and two engravers, Albert Herbert and Dick Fozard, all working away, but another of the artists, Mike Andrews, worried me a little, for, with an apparently unfinished canvas standing in his studio, he was mostly out at parties. I need not have been concerned. He went on to become one of the most well-known post-war painters and in the 1980s I saw the canvas again in his major exhibition in London's Hayward Gallery. It had not changed but I had, having come to realise that a work of art is finished when the artist decides to do no more to it. Knowing when to stop is also vital in the medium I used, for nothing destroys spontaneity and freshness of a watercolour more certainly than overwork.

The painting by Andrews was an evocative image of an Italian friend, Lorenza Mazzetti, a film producer, at the foot of the Spanish Steps. Cinema loomed large in Italy at that time. The most interesting modern design was often to be found in cinema foyers and luxury flats. One day while I was admiring the fine finish and sculptural form of the concrete work on one of these flats near the school a taxi drew up and out stepped the tall beautiful Ingrid Bergman and went in with her shopping bag.

After some weeks' work and daily drives across Rome, I took the director with me to see the building. Ward Perkins had been a Lt Colonel in the North African campaign and no doubt used to travelling in a jeep, which had some resemblance to my little car, for I don't remember him making any comment on it. The tomb, however, greatly interested him and he took many photographs. It was, however, seventeen years in the newly published volume in *The Pelican History of Art* on *Etruscan and Roman Architecture* before I could read his considered opinion of what he had seen for the first time that day:

> the exteriors as have come down to us are remarkable for the exceptional quality of the brickwork (plates 125 and 146) Capitals and entablatures, doorways and window frames, were built up in moulded Terracotta, and the wall-faces themselves were carried out in a brickwork that was special for its decorative qualities and was not uncommonly even treated with a deep crimson slip and picked out along the joints with a hairline of gleaming white plaster.

Both plates referred to are large monochrome photographs of the tomb of Annia Regilla. I still have a tiny fragment of the original crimson colouring that I had found and it amazes me to think that already finely finished multi-coloured brickwork was further embellished. The tomb must originally have gleamed like a large enamelled jewel. But then, the Parthenon, in Herodes Atticus' home city, had its white marble surfaces coloured at the time it was built. My understanding of Annia Regilla's tomb was growing.

Sometimes on a sunny evening I would walk through the gardens beneath the stone pines to the Viale della Trinità dei Monti and past the Villa Medici which housed the French Academy, first of all the schools of art, archaeology and music. Famous names were among its Rome scholars or 'pensionnaires du roi' as they were originally called, including Debussy, who hated his time in Rome and could hardly wait to return to Paris.

Along this route leading to the landmark church of Trinita dei Monti whose striking facade with its two belfries crowns the top of the Spanish Steps, were superb views over the city. At the level of its many domes one looked out across a rich townscape in the mellow golden light. I would sit on a stone bench beside a gentle fountain whose brimful bowl mirrored the evening sky and muse on the historic past and anticipate the immediate future when I was going to spend Christmas with Britt in Vienna.

7   This etching by Wunderlich I bought in Vienna because it captured the atmosphere of the post-war occupied city where Carol Reed's film The Third Man *had just been made.*

VI
CHRISTMAS IN VIENNA

Less than a year after the war in Europe ended I had walked the streets of German cities only defined by the piles of rubble and broken walls on either side. In Rome I had not been conscious of the war but here in Vienna there were still scars.

The previous winter Britt had found lodgings in the zone occupied by the Russians but this winter she had moved into the centre and was staying with the Ondraceks in Margaretenstrasse. 'Mutti' Ondracek who was in charge was like another 'mutti' (Novacek) who Britt already knew. Small, round and caring, these 'muttis' had maternal affection for their guests, including us in the family and spending hours in the kitchen preparing the Austrian dishes which all seemed to be labour intensive.

Britt, however, though just as beautiful, was slimmer than she had been when we parted in Sweden the previous summer 'I only have a roll to eat during the day,' she said, 'I am trying to save money, but that's only when you're not here, älskling. I haven't stopped my teachers coming though. I hope that's alright?' 'That's fine,' I said, 'maybe I can learn something too.' And I did.

Josepha Schramm-Seidl was her voice teacher, and very physical. I heard how the body is simply the singer's instrument and mastery of breath control and correct placement of reverberation in the head to project the tone are essential. Practising diaphragm breathing, lying horizontal, first really filling the lungs, holding the breath with sides distended and then expelling it under control using the lower stomach muscles, is the method and *Rücken füllen* and *Bleib breit!*, were commands I often heard. This, I learned, is something singers practise daily, until it becomes entirely natural and the muscles have strengthened. Then they must maintain it during their singing careers. Josepha was merciless in her assessment of singers and I began to watch out, where costumes allowed me to, for the tell-tale movements of the stomach. Humming to get the reverberation placed rightly was another regular exercise, and then came the speech exercises. There is a notebook somewhere full of them, real tongue twisters.

Being in Vienna was a musical education in itself. The big opera house on the Ringstrasse, the main boulevard around the inner city, had been bombed and burnt during the war, but operas were being given in the much older Theater an der Wien, which had seen many historic performances of Mozart and Strauss. It was relatively small and intimate, had many levels, and we usually sat on a high one. Vienna was surrounded by countries producing marvellous singers and a cast list for *Don Giovanni* included Paul Schöffler, Gottlob Frick, Ljuba Welitsch, Rudolf Schock, Sena Jurinac, Erich Kunz, Hilde Güden, and Walter Berry. We looked down on *Fledermaus*, *Lohengrin* and *Turandot* and knew why the highest level was called 'the Gods'.

For the Christmas season at another theatre was a richly sung *Hansel and Gretel* with Humperdink's music sounding very Wagnerian, and I first heard an Austrian operetta *Die Goldene Meisterin* performed in the authentic style which completely captivated me. I have never heard the like since. The young Fischer-Dieskau, who we had already heard singing Beethoven at the Edinburgh Festival of 1951, was singing Schubert and Schumann song cycles here.

But it was cold! The snow was deep in the streets but the tram lines had been cleared and we could get where we wanted. We travelled on the front platform beside the driver whose mittened hands operated a lever control. The car would swing suddenly left or right as the rails curved into a new direction. The icy wind, the clanging bell and the driver's shouts of *noch jemand zu steigen* are still vivid. At New Year every intersection seemed to have a policeman directing traffic and around his small podium were piled gifts, bottles and boxes prettily wrapped. Vienna seemed to me to have something of a village intimacy about it.

Inside it was cosy. The windows were double; the big glazed tiled stoves radiated heat. We slept in a ground floor room close by one and on New Year's Day, after a party the previous evening, didn't get up until we went out to dine at the nearby Ratskeller. Here, below ground, there was candle light, gleaming tableware, savoury steam and a zither player inevitably playing Anton Karas's *Harry Lime* theme from the recent Carol Reed film set in the shadows of post-war occupied Vienna which surrounded us.

After New Year arrived we had to part yet again but this time we knew we would be meeting at Easter in Venice. Our separations were becoming shorter.

VII

ANNIA REGILLA GROWS UP

Back in Rome at the British School I took up my daily routine of driving across the city and out by Via Appia to reach the temple-like building and continue making the measured notes which would eventually enable me to produce a drawing in colour of its appearance.

And who was the person who had inspired this beautiful building? The full name she was given at her birth, on or around 125 AD already tells a lot about her. Appia Annia Regilla Atilia Caucidia Tertulla indicated, firstly, that among her ancestors was Appius Claudius Caecus who had constructed the most of famous Roman roads in 312 BC.

Regilla means 'little queen' and her family had, indeed, high connections. Through her father she was related to emperors' wives and 'Atilia' referred to descent on her mother's side from an ancient and respected Roman line.

Born into a rich and aristocratic family Annia would have grown up with many slaves around her. Greek wet nurses were especially admired and Annia would no doubt have been raised by one, who may, as many did, have become a life-long friend. In fact, slaves of Greek origin were considered the best baby-tenders precisely because they spoke Greek and came from a civilisation which the Romans much admired. Although Greece had been conquered and now formed part of the Roman Empire its culture was so much admired that in this sense Greece had conquered Rome, and the Roman poet Horace frankly acknowledged: 'Greece, the captive, made her savage victor captive.' Racism, however, was an acceptable feature of Roman society and there was no legal defence against it. Philhellenism or love of all things Greek existed side by side with 'hellenophobia'—hatred of it.

As far as education was concerned Annia was living in an enlightened age. Girls' education was similar to that of boys. As well as hearing Latin and the everyday Greek spoken by the slaves around her a Greek tutor would instruct her in the Greek spoken by the educated upper classes, for it was fashionable in those days to introduce Greek words and phrases into conversation. Her older brother Bradua, who was destined to follow his father into a career in the government, would have been receiving lessons in rhetoric and philosophy, and a curious younger sister would have been able to overhear those given in the house and discuss them with her brother. A library of Greek and Roman books and examples of both Greek and Roman art would be at hand and Annia would have been at ease with Greek language and culture from an early age.

Roman girls also learned to dance as part of their education and it is possible that one of her slaves might have taught her to play the *kithara*—a hand-held seven stringed harp-like instrument. Annia's house might well have resounded to the sound, for a writer of the time criticises a wealthy woman for squandering her money and attention on musicians.

Rome itself, when Annia was growing up, was seeing the completion under Emperor Trajan of a great building programme which had been begun by Augustus, and one of the most remarkable new constructions were the Markets of Trajan, completed just a dozen years or so before Annia was born. An axonometric drawing of its covered market hall had been made by Professor Cordingley and he had asked me to take some check dimensions for him. So I was familiar with the development which Annia, daughter of a well-to-do family, would have been able to visit with her friends and slaves, probably including one as a male bodyguard. The complex was built into the lower slopes of the Quirinal Hill and, as described by Ward Perkins in his survey of the area, was 'an elaborately planned commercial quarter, containing more than one hundred and fifty individual shops and offices, a large covered market hall, linked by stairs and streets and accessible at three different levels … It was the last word in contemporary taste and technique and represents one of the outstanding achievements of the "modern architecture".'

In the second century AD the Roman Empire had reached its largest extent and products would be brought from its farthest corners to supply these markets and provide a choice unsurpassed in the world at that time.

Here Annia would find perfumes and spices, cosmetics and jewellery, embroiderers, shoe shops and textiles of all sorts and colours which she could have made into dresses by expert seamstresses. There would be flower shops with garlands newly prepared for the next banquet her family might be giving, oil and wine shops filled with great amphorae of famous vintages and, of course, food shops of every description.

Whatever special interest Annia had in sport, music or literature she could have found what she wanted here, and there is no reason to doubt that she would have been as interested as today's teenagers are in shopping. Fashion hints were available to her in the pages of Ovid's *Ars Amatoria* where she could read: 'Aurora was clad in saffron but choose your colours with care; they don't suit everyone. Pale skin is best in black. White best sets off a bronzed girl. In white Andromeda charmed Perseus. Clad in white she enticed him to Seriphos.' But regarding cosmetics he warns 'men should be shown out when you put on your make-up.'

In such surroundings and against such a background Annia Regilla would grow into the beautiful and intelligent young woman that an Athenian, the richest man of his time, would choose for his wife.

8 *Herodes Atticus in his sixties. A marble carving in the Louvre. (Photo Courtesy of Herodes Atticus©1989 RMN-Grand Palais/ Herve Lewandowski/The Louvre)*

VIII

HERODES ATTICUS, MULTI-MILLIONAIRE

The size of Herodes' fortune has never been estimated but, as an early biographer commented; the title of millionaire is inadequate to describe a man who constructed all his life monuments of which a single one would have cost several million.

The origin of this wealth lay with his grandfather Hipparchus, was inherited by his son, Atticus, and then, in time, by his elder son called Lucius Vibullius Hipparchus Tiberius Claudius Atticus Herodes. This is Herodes Atticus, husband-to-be of Annia Regilla, and he was born around 101 AD.

He began his literary education early in Athens and, with a rich father, was able to have the best masters. His training would have included the preparation of descriptions, portraits, eulogies or critiques of historic or legendary persons, drawing parallels between great men and writing dissertations on moral issues. There would have been exercises in oratory, for his profession was to be that of a Sophist or 'less highly regarded' that of a lawyer. The Sophists would read or extemporise a discourse at festivals, marriages, birthdays, civic welcomes or funerals. In this second period of sophism, eloquence had been transformed into an intellectual sport, concentrating on form and virtuosity of execution. Interest was focused on the personality of the orator and an acting talent would be an advantage. Herodes obviously had an aptitude and became perhaps the best known Sophist of the time and a sought-after teacher in his turn.

This, however, was not enough for Herodes, realising that his art was ephemeral, and, in fact, there is no discourse surviving which can be securely attributed to him. His other activity was as a patron of architecture, using his wealth to create needed structures which would ensure lasting fame. It is indeed the patron, the enabler, rather than the architect who is remembered from those times. Pericles gets the credit for the Parthenon as it was his vision and management that brought it into being although he was not the designer or sculptor.

Herodes was fluent in Latin and would have learnt it when living in Rome as part of the household of Calvisius Tullus, a consul. In this cultivated milieu the daughter of his host, Domitia Lucilla, was interested in Greek, and she was to become the mother of Marcus Aurelius. Later we know that the young Marcus Aurelius was being taught by Herodes around 143, and they became friends.

Whether or not Herodes met Annia Regilla during the period he was living in the consul's household we do not know. Perhaps he had visited the Appia family and had noticed a charming and talented eight-year-old, as Robert Schumann had first noticed Clara without dreaming that when she was fifteen they would kiss for the first time. In these matters we have no evidence but only our knowledge of the human heart to help us imagine how Annia and Herodes' relationship began, and what they felt for each other when they married in 138 or 139 AD.

Regilla's parents, however, were doubtless pleased when Herodes chose their daughter, although considering the great difference between the fortunes they would hardly have taken the initiative in suggesting the union. The legal minimum age for Roman girls to marry was twelve and motherhood was expected by the age of twenty. Marriage was based on the consent of both parties, although it may have been previously arranged. At this time Annia Regilla was thirteen or fourteen years old and may already have had suitors, and have seen her friends marrying young men in their twenties. However, the fact that Herodes was some twenty-four years older than his bride was by no means unusual in Rome, and Annia could see before her a man who offered her the possibility of a life more interesting than that of a politician or military man's wife. She would know about Herodes as a teacher of rhetoric and patron of the arts. Perhaps they had musical interests in common? She was fluent in Greek and marrying an Athenian, far from presenting problems, would bring a new dimension to her life.

As can be seen from a carving now in the Louvre, Herodes in his sixties was still a handsome man. In his late thirties he may well have been irresistible, for the famous Sophists were the equivalent of pop-stars in their time. Annia, although no likeness of her has survived, for all the remaining statues are headless, must have been beautiful. This we know because Herodes, as the evidence of the building he created in her memory proves, was a lover of beauty. He had, of course, no need to marry for money, and although marriage into a highly connected Roman family gave status, there would have been alternatives. That he chose Annia indicates a particular attraction.

The only cloud on the horizon was possibly some jealousy on the part of her brother Bradua. Not every Roman was a lover of Greek culture or the way they had been given top jobs including teachers of rhetoric. There is a reference to Herodes being called a 'Graeculus' or 'little Greek' an unflattering racial stereotype created by Juvenal. Racism was the downside of Roman pride. There would come a time when Bradua and Herodes would be in open conflict, but this was some decades ahead.

IX

THE ROMAN NECROPOLIS BENEATH ST PETER'S

As I worked round the external walls of Annia's temple/tomb I often wondered what it had looked like inside. The remaining surfaces of the vaulted interior were just rough concrete. The finishes, plaster, mosaic, whatever they were, had been removed. A unique opportunity, however, came to me to see how the interior would have matched the exterior in its beauty.

Excavations in the crypt of St Peter's during and immediately after the war had led to the discovery of a Roman cemetery beneath it. The roofs of the tombs had been removed and the interiors earth-filled in order that the altar of Constantine's first church could be located over the precise spot where, it was believed, the remains of St Peter had rested in a wall shrine. These excavations by the Vatican archaeologists had continued for more than ten years and had finally been published in December 1951 in a large and costly official report.

The British School's director, Ward Perkins, was now engaged on a book to make these fascinating discoveries available to a wider reading public and, in early 1954, was needing drawing assistance in preparing plans and diagrams for the volume entitled *The Shrine of St Peter* eventually published by Longmans, Green & Co. in 1956. I was recruited to make the first drafts of two plans showing the layout of tombs in relation to the church above, and in payment I would be able to extend my time in Rome, for I was on a limited scholarship sum. More importantly, I was able to visit the excavations, some thirty feet below the floor of St Peter's. Special permission was needed, for the space among the tombs is too confined and the stucco, painting and mosaic decoration too delicate for the general public ever to be admitted.

After descending a staircase, the necropolis or 'city of the dead' is reached and the house tombs revealed—buildings which had not been seen for sixteen centuries. They are, as the plans show, closely grouped with little or no space between them and like Annia's temple/tomb are generally square vaulted chambers built of concrete and faced externally with very thin, rose-coloured bricks with layers of fine mortar between. The exteriors however, are not the focus. It is the interiors with their vaulted roofs and elaborate decorations which are.

9   'One afternoon I took time off to relax and sketched the fig tree growing against the nearby brick wall.' *Ink drawing by John Graham.*

Most, if not all, of the tombs were built between 125 AD, when Annia was born, and the end of the second century and their interiors are therefore contemporary with the one which Herodes would have created, perhaps using some of the same craftsmen and artists.

I have vivid memories of these interiors, which had emerged with their colours remarkably fresh from their earth packaging. In one, the range was polychromatic—a purple plinth above a black and white floor surmounted by walls of greenish blue or Pompeian red with contrasting white architectural detailing. Walls and ceilings were generally stucco-covered and the motifs ranged from rosettes to leaf sprays, landscapes, birds, fishes and figures. All was remarkably lively and it seemed to suggest the world in which the departed had lived or the paradise they could anticipate. Venus arising from the sea suggested a rebirth. As Ward Perkins wrote: 'the Vatican housetombs, so simple without, so richly decked and colourful within, were surely regarded as places in which the dead, in some sense or at some time, resided.'

Now I could imagine the rough-walled interior of the building I was measuring, as a finely crafted colourful kaleidoscope celebrating Annia's life.

There was to be no snow that winter in Rome. Perhaps there rarely is? The measuring was going well and its end was in sight. One afternoon I took time off to relax and sketched the fig tree growing against the nearby brick wall. It was still leafless but the sun was getting stronger each day. I bought sprays of mimosa to have in my studio and the special scent from its tiny yellow balls of blossom can always transport me back to these times.

At Easter I would be meeting Britt in Venice.

10 *Palazzo da' Mosto painted by John Graham on a first visit to Venice in 1951.*

11 *Photograph by Dick Felton of the artist at work.*

X

ENGAGEMENT IN VENICE

It was not my first visit to Venice. I had been there by London taxi at Easter two years previously. Indeed, that experience of driving on the continent had encouraged me to undertake the drive to Rome. It was not, however, without mishap.

The taxi belonged to Dick Felton who was studying town planning at Manchester University but through his interests in photography and architecture we had met and become friends. A team of three architectural students was enlisted to join him for the drive to Venice during the 1951 Easter vacation.

I don't remember the age or make of the vehicle but it was a large black and upright typical London taxi, very roomy in the back and with additional fold-down seats. The driver had space beside him for luggage and a glass partition behind, with a sliding panel for passenger communication. The body, unusually I thought, was made of aluminium. Three of us had driving licences. Dick had driven in the army, but I had only recently passed my test, and during the trip the distance driven on the right was to exceed the distance I had so far driven on the left. Dick organised everything.

We were across the Channel and making good progress when the crash occurred. Foolishly, we had decided to continue driving after it got dark and that was our mistake. Neither Dick nor I were driving when we pulled in behind a slow-moving lorry to avoid an oncoming car over a railway bridge, only to be poleaxed by a load of steel bars projecting from the lorry and marked only by a tied-on rag. Our radiator was pushed in and the lower part of the windscreen smashed. Nobody was hurt and the lorry soon continued on its way but it looked as though our trip was finished. We pushed the taxi over the bridge and slept in it.

When we awakened on Good Friday morning we found we were beside a garage. Its owner said little when he came out but adjusted his beret, drew on his Gauloise, and then sent two of us off to a scrapyard in the nearby town with dimensions of a French radiator that would fit. Meanwhile,

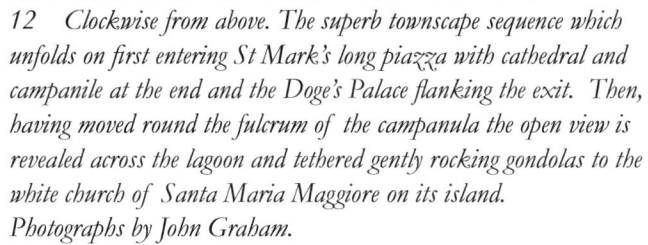

12 Clockwise from above. The superb townscape sequence which unfolds on first entering St Mark's long piazza with cathedral and campanile at the end and the Doge's Palace flanking the exit. Then, having moved round the fulcrum of the campanula the open view is revealed across the lagoon and tethered gently rocking gondolas to the white church of Santa Maria Maggiore on its island.
Photographs by John Graham.

he began repairs on the fan blades. Before Easter Monday we were moving again, sporting a classy Delage radiator, which led Dick to christen his taxi 'Daisy Delage' and minus a chunk of our holiday 'spends' but with the *entente cordiale* greatly strengthened.

I had decided to do a large painting in Venice and, as luggage space was no problem, had brought a sheet of Whatman paper pre-stretched on a wooden board. For my subject I selected a palazzo on the Grand Canal which was not one of the famous ones but showed a degree of neglect and, with its additions and blend of Byzantine and Renaissance elements, formed a fascinating composition. It would have to sum up my first experience of Venice. The sun shone on my subject, but the opposite side of the canal where I sat it was cold and, close to a fish market, smelly. Steps down to the water provided a good working spot. Dick took the photograph.

Just as the time with Britt in Vienna had furthered our musical education, this Easter in Venice did as much for art. That education, for Britt, had begun in hospital where she spent several years after an attack of polio as a teenager. Unable to continue schooling she had, as soon as she was able to read again, chosen to study English language and literature and art history. No subjects could have been more appropriate considering the life we were to lead together.

We visited the Scuolas adorned with paintings and frescoes; the Belle Arte Museum with its perfect Bellinis, and lost ourselves frequently in the labyrinth of alleyways. Venice itself was like a series of stage sets; its many small squares providing scenes for the walk-on characters to talk and gesticulate. Their speech and footfalls echoed from the surrounding walls and this together with the cooing of pigeons formed a continuous noise, punctuated by great clashes of bells every hour or so.

Our small *pensionne* in a side street near St Mark's was, I remember, called Anima Bella ('beautiful soul') and we discovered veal in Marsala to be one of our favourite dishes. If the institution of marriage had not existed we would have invented it, for we wanted to be together always. A diamond engagement ring on a Rome Scholar's allowance was not within reach but in a tiny jeweller's window we found a milky opal which was already heart-shaped and had it simply set in gold.

Painting was not this time on the agenda but I had the Kine-Exakta twin lens reflex camera I had acquired in Germany with me and I took many photographs. In particular I tried to record the superb townscape sequence which unfolded on first entering St Mark's long piazza with the cathedral and campanile at the far end and the Doge's Palace flanking the exit. Then, having moved round the fulcrum of the campanile, the open view was revealed across the lagoon and tethered gently rocking gondolas to the white church of Santa Maria Maggiore on its island.

13a, b   Britt aboard the ferry to Chioggia and below, the view from it.

One day we took a ferry trip down the lagoon to Chioggia. As we sat waiting to depart I photographed Britt and then the gondolas below the stern waiting for passengers. At Murano we watched coloured glass being blown and in little Burano's great church wondered at the wall-to-wall Last Judgement filling its east end.

Venice was a dreamlike fantasy in which everything had its watery equivalent and its existence seemed to cease as one left.

14 A renaissance composition. I had yet to visit Rome when I produced this Renaissance Composition in my final year at Manchester University. The buildings which include some of Rome's most famous, are accurately shown and shadows rendered by up to twenty washes of Chinese ink but the composition is my own and never existed.

XI

IN ROME AND THE CAMPAGNA

We arrived at Rome by train and came out of what was the finest modern station in Europe, built with the sculptural bravura with which the Italians were then using reinforced concrete. The great projecting canopy's curve over the entrance concourse reflected the shape of the part of the surviving city wall which flanked it—an example of Rome's constant dialogue with its past.

Britt was allowed to stay at the British School. Since then, however, I have learnt that the School's policy towards wives or partners in the past had been very different. In 1923 Professor Cordingley, then the Rome Scholar in architecture, had married the School's assistant librarian but she had not been allowed to move in. Later the governing Committee had relented when John Skeaping, who held the Rome Scholarship in Sculpture from 1924-27 met and married Barbara Hepworth, who was on a travelling scholarship from the West Riding. They moved into the School in the summer of 1925. In his autobiography of 1977 Skeaping writes: 'We bought a lot of tropical birds, pigeons and a monkey. I taught Barbara to carve marble ... we were blissfully happy ... I carved a portrait direct in marble of Barbara, which was the best work I had done to date.' It is interesting for me to think of Barbara Hepworth learning her stone carving at the British School for two years previously at the delightful Festival of Britain I had seen her sculpture *Contrapuntal Forms* dominating the central space on the South Bank site between the huge Dome of Discovery and the Transport Pavilion. It was doubly unusual at the time for being by a woman, and for being carved in its blue limestone directly by the hand of the artist rather than by assistants. At the close of the exhibition it came to the new town of Harlow and I can reflect that as a member of Harlow Art Trust I share responsibility for its care, as it is one of the most important pieces in the collection which we have placed throughout the town.

Britt and I did not import any pigeons into the School, but we did invite friends to dinner, having previously informed Bruno, of course. This was a nice thing one could do and it added another dimension to our small community. I remember one evening when composer Menotti had been invited and talked about the festival he was starting at Spoleto. We visited an Italian artist, Javarone,

15a Termini Station. The result of a national competition held in 1947.

b. The flats where Ingrid Bergman lived.

c.   Rome as I saw it.

d.   Taking tea on the steps of the British School.

who lived in what had been an *ucelleria* ('aviary') and sat with his wife and two delightful daughters in their sunny garden. The Javarones were one of several Christian Science contacts I had been given by Britt's friends in London, where she had regularly attended church and had been helped by a practitioner, Geith Plimmer, to gain greater freedom in walking. I had also been to services and lectures and read, but it was not until I was alone in Rome that I began to think seriously about it. There was a Christian Science Society, founded after the war, which held services in a room close to the tiny Borromini church of San Carlo alle Quattro Fontane and I began to attend. There were often American visitors and on one occasion I sat next to Ginger Rogers.

Founded on primitive Christianity—the words and works of Christ Jesus—before church organisation and doctrinal definitions took over, it made sense to me in its radical simplicity, and still does.

As sightseers in Rome in 1954 Britt and I saw it very much as it appears in the film *Roman Holiday* which was made on location the previous year, when Audrey Hepburn was the same age as Britt, and every time I see this classic film it brings back the sights and sounds of the city exactly as it was then. We looked up the great sweep of the Spanish Steps; put our hands, not without a tremor, into the 'la Bocca della verita'. Our favourite fountain, however, was the less frequented Fontana delle Tararughe in its small piazza, where four graceful bronze boys hold dolphins delivering water and tiny tortoises drink from the fountain bowl they support.

A favourite museum was the Villa Guilia's display of Etruscan work which was quite close to the British School. We admired the famous sarcophagus of the 'Bride and Bridegroom': a young couple reclining together on a banqueting couch, the man's hand laid on his wife's shoulder. Their expressions were gentle. Nothing is known of their names, or why, as it appears, they died together so young in the sixth century BC. There was evidence in Etruscan culture of a passion for music and dancing—the flute, zither and lyre being often seen in their paintings—and in Roman times, it seems, the flautists at the ritual of temple sacrifices were always Etruscans.

We drove to Tivoli to see the fountains in the gardens of the Villa d'Este and to Ostica Antica on the coast where recent excavations had exposed what was, after Pompeii and Herculaneum, the finest remains of a Roman town. It certainly had an impressive and very public toilet where Britt graciously posed for a photograph.

 We were also photographed on the steps of the British School, taking tea. It was the young waiter Enrico, responding, as so many did, to Britt's charm who had brought tea to us where we sat in the sun.

We went out to the Campagna, where I showed Britt the building I had been measuring and told her what I knew about Annia and Herodes at that time. In the School's library I had found a reference in Thomas Ashby's *The Roman Campagna in Classical Times* (Benn, London, 1927):

> Further down the valley towards Rome, standing in a farmyard, is a picturesque brick tomb, finely decorated on the outside with columns and cornices in cut brick, of great elegance in design; while the use of yellow bricks in combination with the dark red gives a very beautiful colour effect. It is thought by Lanciani e Lughi to have been the tomb of Annia Regilla, and though the interior will be seen, by those who penetrate into what is now a fowl house, to be faced with brickwork of far less careful construction the identification will probably stand. It is generally known as the temple of the Deus Rediculus, but there is of course no warrant for the name.

Nearly thirty years later it was still 'a fowl house' and wrongly identified in the current guidebook.

We did not explore the Campagna further. In these early post-war years it was still largely uncultivated and neglected. Even ten years later in 1965 when Georgina Masson's guide to Rome was published she could write lyrically of the nearby so-called 'Egeria's Grotto' which had been a place of pilgrimage for artists and writers in the sixteenth century, 'a rough path leads across the fields down into the valley; the ruins of ancient terraces are barely discernible under the brambles; rushes whisper in the bed of an invisible stream whose rippling fills the still air. At the bottom we turned left along the old farm road, overgrown with grass and bushes; suddenly we see a real classical grotto, with a spring of clear ice-cold water gushing from a niche, just as it must have done for centuries … no one ever seems to come here now; the wilderness which surrounds it has preserved it inviolate; it is to the hoped that it will long continue to do so … '

It has always been an area of natural beauty and peace, but when Annia and Herodes lived here in the second century it would have been part of a well-run family estate.

XII

ANNIA AND HERODES' EARLY MARRIED YEARS

The buildings which already existed on the Appia family estate would be improved to suit the comfort and tastes of the newlyweds and we can be sure that with their resources nothing would be lacking. Here was a welcome refuge from the noisy, hot and occasionally disease-ridden city and a relief from its political, and possibly professional, intrigue. It would be an excellent environment for their children, but all was not to prove idyllic.

Regilla's first child was born within a year of their marriage but died shortly afterwards. This was not unusual, for at that time two thirds of children died in their first year and, in Rome, children who died before the age of ten were not to be lamented publically. There are, however, two letters known to have been written concerning this death. Marcus Aurelius wrote to his older friend and former teacher, Cornelius Fronto; 'Herodes' son born (today) has died. Herodes is not bearing this with equanimity. I would like you to write a few words to him about this event.' Fronto's subsequent letter to Herodes reads, in part, 'For there is no aspect of your age that prevents you from rearing other children. Every loss is difficult if hope is cut off, but easier if some hope remains of recovery.' This rather cool letter expresses the stoic view and, in their Roman eyes, Herodes expression of grief seemed over-emotional. Herodes, however, was not a follower of the stoic philosophy and his expression of feeling shows that Annia did not have a cold and reserved husband, far from it. Herodes seems to have been a passionate man, active and ambitious.

A memoir by a young student from the years in Athens gives a fascinating insight into his views:

> I once heard the consular Herodes Atticus speaking at length, in Greek, in which language he was outstanding among all men of our time in the seriousness, fluency and elegance of his diction. He was speaking at the time against the 'lack of feeling' of the Stoics—their belief that emotions should be kept in check. The emotional Herodes could not accept this attitude and compared the Stoics with an ignorant barbarian, who having learned that pruning is good, proceeds to chop down all his vines and olives. 'Thus,' said Herodes, 'these disciples of the cult of the unemotional, who want

to be considered calm, brave and steadfast because they show neither desire nor grief, neither anger nor pleasure, cut out the more active emotions of the spirit and grow old in torpor, a sluggish, enervated life.'

There is another episode from his earlier life which throws light on his character and and also on the character of his friend Marcus Aurelius which is also to prove significant in view of a much later event concerning Annia.

When quite a young man Herodes was made administrator of the free cities of Asia. The Emperor Antoninus had a high opinion of Herodes as a man of high character and princely generosity but it seems that during his rule he made bitter enemies and an Athenian deputation made accusations against him and brought about a trial, at which Herodes defended himself successfully to the satisfaction of the emperor. Fronto was involved, apparently having accepted a brief for the prosecution, and had written to Marcus Aurelius for advice. He was concerned that the charges included spoliation, violence and murder, and Fronto writes that he is willing to let some of these drop 'if it be the prince's pleasure.' Marcus Aurelius, however, flatly rejects the suggestion and states 'all that concerns the case you are supporting must be clearly brought forward.'

In requiring that his friend is not given special treatment but a fair trial on the merits of the case, Aurelius is being completely consistent with what we know of his character, which is a great deal. Unique among the emperors he recorded his inmost thoughts gathered into twelve books known as his *Meditations* which have been taken, due to their high principles, as a guide to conduct for many during the succeeding centuries.

It is relevant to note that Aurelius wrote his *Meditations* in Greek, a further example of the closeness of Greek and Roman culture.

There would be much to do on this large estate and large numbers of slaves to do the work. Looking back on these times Herodes refers to 'broad fields, rows of cultivated vines and acres of olive trees'. It was clearly, as he calls it, a 'fruitful estate'. Herodes, however, cared about his position in posterity and was, no doubt, aware that his highly regarded teaching and oratory was not the stuff likely to survive, as has proved to be the case, and he would seek to make his mark in other ways and for that Greece would be the scene for his activities.

A second child was born within two years and the Greek name given to their daughter—Elpinice—may be a sign that a journey was being contemplated.

Britt and I were also soon to leave Rome and travel south.

XIII

TO SICILY IN SEARCH OF VIKINGS

The end of my scholarship time was approaching and we decided on a major excursion before leaving Italy. A guide book in the British School Library described Sicily as 'the world's most beautiful and most interesting island' and on the way we could see Pompeii and the Greek temples at Paestum. We were also offered accommodation by one of the artists who had rented a little house by the sea near Cefalù. But there was another reason.

Britt came from the southern part of Sweden which, until less than four hundred years previously, had been part of Denmark, whose Viking expeditions in the eighth and ninth centuries had been towards England and the Frankish world. These Vikings founded Normandy. Their subsequent invasion and settlement in England was, of course, well known to me, but the fact that during the same period (1130-1194) they had established the kingdom of Sicily was intriguing. The motives for such a far flung expedition were various but they must also have been inspired by a spirit of adventure, as we were. It would be interesting to see what, if any, legacy they had left.

We set off on a very hot June day with waiter Enrico and two artist-engravers posing for the departure photograph from the foot of the British School entrance stairway. Through the Pincian gardens we drove down to the Piazza Populo, between the two churches into the Corso, and then out to Rome by the Porto San Sebastiano onto the ancient Via Appia. This time we did not turn off toward the Regilla estate but continued south along the old road, lined with tombs and the occasional umbrella pine until Rome was far behind us.

The sea was out of sight on our right and the road was level if not always smooth. Sometime that afternoon we gave a lift to a charming young man whose very plausible hard-luck story relieved us of part of our cash. It was supposed to be a loan, for we would be returning that way, but even then we suspected we should never be paid back, and we were proved right.

After he departed, however, we were soon in Pompeii, amid the extensive town ruins backed by the distant hills all bathed in golden late afternoon light and I had my Exakta in my hands.

16   The Doric Temples at Paestum

17   The extensive ruins of Pompeii

That night we stayed at a small hotel in Vico Equense towards Sorrento which had been recommended by one of the School staff. The window of our pleasant room overlooked a vine-covered pergola and beneath it flickered the images of a film being shown in the courtyard, accompanied by the subdued sounds of the Italian dialogue. It was a windless, warm evening and the waters of the Gulf of Naples moved below.

The next day we reached Paestum and I had one of the great architectural experiences of my life. The power and beauty of the well preserved Greek temples was a revelation. The porous texture of the stone even increased their grandeur and the siting between the sea and the hills was particularly beautiful. I took many photographs and then, although it was time to move on, I was driven to paint. This was the first but not the last of several Greek sites we were to visit and wonder at the partnership between man's building and nature, which was, for the Greeks, the home of their gods.

When we reached the campsite where we intended to stop the night, simply using our sleeping bags beside the car, other campers were putting up tents and we heard German accents.

The guardian of the place took pity on us and insisted that we come into his house. Perhaps we would have preferred sleeping out, but his kindness was irresistible and remains unforgettable. We slept on the floor while the family including several children were all together in the next room. Newspapers covered the walls and there were no furnishings, yet they insisted on giving us cocoa in the morning before we left.

The mountains of southern Italy are not spectacular but they attain respectable altitudes, and although gradients may not be steep they are very, very long. It seemed we had been climbing all afternoon. The sun beat down from a cloudless sky on an uncultivated landscape where there was nothing to moderate the heat nor any human habitation in sight.

I could hear the radiator boiling and suddenly the car seized up and stopped. I knew what had happened. A couple of the many bolts around the oil sump were missing and as I had not been able to find replacements I had substituted corks.

With the uninterrupted long vibration of the climb the corks had loosened and been lost, together with the oil. I visualised the swollen pistons locked tight in their cylinders.

Britt, meanwhile, was looking into her small copy of the words-only edition of the Christian Science Hymnal, as she often did. I got out, put in new corks, fresh oil and, when boiling subsided, topped up the radiator. But starting was another matter. The starter handle, however hard I tried, produced no movement. Physical force, anyway, as I had learnt is never the answer. In the past, starting had sometimes been achieved by running backwards in neutral and then engaging reverse gear. So I this I tried, but the car jerked to a stop as though an ultra-efficient brake had been applied. But had I detected a slight movement?

I tried again, and again, and again—each time noticing more movement, while Britt read quietly on. Eventually, the engine was working freely by the sound of it. I engaged forward gear and we proceeded to climb the long slope again. There was no stopping this time and no sign ever after that the car had suffered such a seizure.

In the evening we paused in a small village to enquire about somewhere to stay, and immediately a crowd surrounded us. We were told we would be guided somewhere, and a young man began to untie our rucksack from the back of the car—unnecessarily I thought. The situation was getting out of hand so I turned the car around and without looking back, waved farewell. It was not yet dark when we came down from the hills to a town with a hotel. It was new, characterless and ugly, but safe.

The next day we reached the Straits of Messina and crossed by ferry to Sicily. We turned left to Taormina; climbed the winding road up to it from the coast and came into the town square as it got dark. A small crowd gathered as we enquired about accommodation. I must have mentioned the Mafia for someone said, 'Oh we're all Mafia here' and they laughed …

18   The interior of one of the Doric Temples at Paestum

19 'goats with long, sharp twisted horns gazed at us as we drove by …'

20   *With Britt outside the house by the sea in Cefalù*

XIV

IN SICILY

We may well have been staying with a Mafia grandmother but we were comfortably looked after and treated to a succession of succulent risottos—our favourite Italian dish. It was good to relax after our days of driving.

Taormina, on its platform 700ft above the sea, contained much beauty. The small weather-beaten mansions in its streets showed details blending Saracenic and Gothic styles which I sketched. In the surrounding country goats with long, sharp, twisted horns gazed at us as we drove by among bushes of cactus and spurge. Tall spikes of acanthus and aloe thrived in semi-tropical sunshine. The midday heat was merciless and the limestone towns capping the hills were bleached white.

Most beautiful of all was the theatre on Taormina's eastern side. Here the semicircle of seating could accommodate thousands and a voice from the stage would be heard by all. The ruins we could see were Roman but the original theatre had been built on this site chosen by the Greeks and erected in the second century AD which was the time in which Annia and Herodes lived. The Greek siting was breathtakingly beautiful. Behind the scenic building the sea formed a bay beyond which the land sloped upward to the snow covered summit of Mount Etna with its constant plume of volcanic steam. Truly a setting for plays about the gods.

Our next destination was Cefalù on the north coast and again it was dark when we reached the end of the day's journey. I found the turning off to the house where we were to stay but it was little more than a track down a grassy slope towards the sea. After a while I decided it was too dangerous to continue in complete darkness. We stopped, took out the bench seat together with its back and, propping them against the warm radiator, ate our supper by the light of the tiny sidelights. Way down below, out on the sea, moved fishing boats with phosphorus lanterns projecting out over their prows. It was a still summer night and we used our sleeping bags beside the car. When dawn came we could see the little white house at the end of the track not far below.

21   The Norman cathedral built in the twelfth century by King Roger stands at the back of Cefalù immediately below the huge cliff

22   The mosaics in the apse, executed in 1148 by Arab craftsmen and considered 'the most splendid in Sicily'

The great twelfth-century Norman cathedral stood at the back of nearby Cefalù, at the foot of the great cliff-like rock which dominates the town. Build in creamy limestone it rose high above the other buildings and looked a typical Normandy composition with the tall towers of its entrance front linked by an arcaded facade in three tiers.

It had been founded in 1131 by King Roger following a vow he made when returning to Sicily and in danger of shipwreck, Cefalù being the place he came safely to land. At this date the kingdom had been established for some time, the conquest of Sicily having taken thirty years from 1060 to 1091. That conquest was accomplished by two brothers, Robert and Roger who came from the relatively minor Hauteville family in Normandy, at more or less the same time that the conquest of England was being undertaken by William, descendant of a line of dukes. The Hauteville brothers, however, belonged to lower aristocracy and being younger sons had to seek their fortunes elsewhere while two thirds of the inheritance went to the older brother. Italy being a rich country with fine landscapes and monuments attracted these adventurers and they had been active in the south for several years before they responded to a Muslim emir's appeal for support and landed in Sicily in 1060.

The large part of the island's population at that time were Muslims with a small minority of Christians, Greeks and others. From the outset the Normans respected the different religions on the island and for a long time Arabic was the main language. Sicily, under the Normans, appears to have been a multicultural and multilingual island. The building expertise that the Normans brought with them had created great cathedrals and castles in England often using the fine stone imported from Normandy. Here in Sicily, however, they had a plentiful local stone in which to build this impressive structure in a style familiar to me.

The interior, on the other hand, was a complete surprise. The entire east end was covered in mosaics, dating from 1148, telling the Christian story. Here was the equivalent of the stained glass windows of Canterbury's Norman cathedral in Byzantine style mosaics executed by Arab craftsmen. Our guide book said that they were 'certainly the most splendid in Sicily' and as we gazed at the great image of the Saviour which filled the semi-dome of the apse we saw a face which was not reminiscent of classical but of eastern models, and all the more appropriate for being so. Mary, the prophets, apostles, saints and elders were all represented in gleaming colour and clear design. In the blazing sunlight of Sicily small windows were the rule, and wall mosaic was a brilliant solution. Furthermore, the Normans had created a church where Christians and Arabs could feel at home.

Sixty years on, when the world is bedevilled by polarization of peoples along national, ethnic, and religious lines, these Sicilian churches set a remarkable example of reconciliation, and it is

23   The author's photograph from the Greek ruins of Solunto attained after a climb of 600ft.

ironic to think that it was set by descendants of the Vikings whose popular reputation is as pagan plunderers. Even today 'King Robert' is affectionately regarded in Sicily. We had certainly found a legacy left by the Normans.

Between Cefalù and Palermo was the site of the former Phoenician, later Roman, town of Solunto. A climb of 600ft to the height where the terraced streets and a few ruins were to be found provided the anticipation which was then rewarded by a view along the coast to the mountains. 'Scarcely surpassed by anything in Sicily.' Again we were enchanted as at Paestum and Taormina. Sometimes the beauty of the siting speaks as eloquently as the ruins that remain.

It was time to leave the island. We had never been threatened or in danger, but somehow I sensed a violence beneath the surface of daily life and this was in my mind as I sat on the rocks beside the little house on one of the last days and painted the turbulent sea. Still today, Sicily stands somewhat apart from the other islands of the Mediterranean because of the Mafia.

On our return journey we did not have to face the mountains again, but with our remaining money bought a boat passage from Palermo to Naples. From here it was but a morning's drive to Rome. A return of our loan at the agreed rendezvous would have been welcome but, as we now anticipated, was not forthcoming. With a rudimentary petrol gauge I wondered if we had enough petrol to make it, and coasted down hills when possible. We did, however, arrive in time to catch lunch, but when I later went out to park the car it wouldn't start. Removing the petrol cap I could see the bottom of the tank—bone dry.

24   The turbulent Sicilian sea. Painting by John Graham.

Die Akropolis von Athen.

25   This drawing of the Acropolis as Annia Regilla may have seen it when she arrived from Rome in the second century AD was given to the author in a portfolio of German archaeological reconstructions when spending Christmas with Britt in Vienna with the Ondracek family. They knew I was studying to be an architect but the story of Annia and Herodes was yet to unfold.

XV
ANNIA AND HERODES MOVE TO ATHENS

Following the birth of their second child; a daughter to whom they gave the Greek name Elpinice, Annia and Herodes would enjoy the beauty and fruitfulness of the Appia estate for a while. But there came a time when 'the voice of Athens' needed to return to his native city where he would have scope for his building activities.

In marrying Herodes Annia knew that she would not be leading the life of a typical Roman aristocratic wife married to a politician or a soldier; but that new horizons would open for her. Young unmarried upper-class Roman men could travel to complete their education: a sort of 'Grand Tour' of the time, but young women were not free to do so. The journey, when Elpinice was old enough to travel, may well have been eagerly anticipated by Annia.

Travelling south, even with the best comfort money could buy, still meant long, bumpy days in covered carriages with solid wheels. Annia, however, could take her personal slaves with her, including nurses and attendants for little Elpinice and perhaps even personal friends.

Their destination in Italy, before embarking from Brindisi by sea for Greece, was another Appia family estate in Apulia. As they passed Naples and turned towards the Adriatic coast they would see the peak of Mount Vesuvius. No doubt the disaster which had engulfed Pompeii in 79 AD—only sixty years or so previously—would have been in their minds, having read the vivid eye-witness accounts by Pliny the Younger, but the area, still deep in ash, was to be avoided.

Arriving after many days travel at the family estate in Canusium (modern Canosa) Annia was frustrated to find a dry and dusty place without sufficient water to be able to give her little girl a decent wash. The once prosperous town had been on the wrong side in a war in the first century BC, had lost favour with Rome, and its decline had been hastened by water scarcity. Herodes, man of action, proceeded to endow the town with an enormous aqueduct bringing water from over twenty miles away. This was obviously not the work of a moment but the decision to build would have been taken at this time, and Annia would have been involved because of her important family contacts. Eventually the city was to be restored to Roman favour and prosperity, and Herodes was credited with this revitalisation. It was a period when not only kings and emperors but wealthy citizens could be patrons of public works and Herodes was one of the greatest of these. At the Panathenaic Festival in 139/40 AD he had promised a stadium to the Athenians and it was achieved, in marble, by the next festival in 143/44. Probably for its inauguration, with his young wife beside him, Herodes was now travelling to Athens.

Coming from Rome, that great hub of a vast empire, would Annia have been disappointed on first seeing Herodes' city? Some have thought so. The Athens before her eyes was built on a plain backed by mountains and surrounded by the blue waters of the Saronic Gulf. It was dominated by a huge limestone rock forming a natural fortress crowned by marble temples. These were painted in bright colours and although the city had suffered much depredation in the centuries since the Golden Age under Pericles it was now witnessing a new flowering supported by Roman emperors such as Hadrian and citizens such as Herodes.

Its conquest by Rome in 146 BC had been followed by a spiritual conquest in reverse. Rome remained the centre of the empire and its largest city, but Athens was, in a sense, its cultural capital. Young Roman members of the aristocracy came to complete their education in its philosophical schools and libraries. Among them would be friends and acquaintances of Herodes and Annia.

Contrasting this city with the Rome she had left which, despite its magnificence, was also full of crowded high-rise blocks, narrow smelly streets, and the unending activity of new construction and goods traffic, she would have appreciated the quieter tempo, the sea breezes and the unique beauty of its setting. Not 'surely' a disappointment to her.

Moreover, as cities reflect the values and resolve of their citizens, so Athens differed from Rome. The mass, bloodthirsty spectacles of the Colosseum were not to the Athenian taste; drama and music were. The agora, the temples, the stadium, the theatre and the public spaces of Athens were an expression of their culture and the stages for its development. This was reflected in the oath taken by new citizens. 'We will leave this city not less but greater, better and more beautiful than it was left to us.' It was an oath which Herodes, now in partnership with Annia Regilla, would amply fulfil.

In achieving his projects Herodes would need to be wealthy patron, part architect and builder rolled into one; to be well connected and to make use of his persuasive talents. He would also need to entertain, and as head of his household it was Annia's duty to arrange this and to be a good hostess. It was a role natural to her for she had grown up in an aristocratic family with a father who was a consul. She would have observed her mother being a hostess and, as the only daughter, would have been closely involved. Perhaps when Herodes and Annia first met she may have been assisting her mother in this way and have attracted his attention?

In addition to a house near Athens such a wealthy family would doubtless have had a seaside property, but wherever they lived there would surely have been no shortage of water; water to bring on exotic fruits and luxuriant foliage in their gardens; water to supply fountains and pools and of what might have been a mini-Alhambra.

The style in which Herodes lived in the years even before his marriage to Annia can be gathered from a student admirer of his, Aulus Gellius, writing in his *Attic Nights* :

> Herodes Atticus the consular of true Greek eloquence, often invited me to his country home hear the city, with senator Servilianus and several other Romans who had come to Greece from Rome in search of culture. At that time, when we were there at his villa called Cephisia, we used to be protected against the unpleasant heat in summer of the burning autumn sun by shade of his spacious groves, long cool avenues and the cool position of the house. It had elegant baths with abundance of sparkling waters and as a whole was a charming place, with a melodious sound of running water and birdsong.

The dominant element of the house would have been a large centrally light hall, the atrium, with the other rooms grouped around it. In polite society one took food from a table while reclining on one's left elbow on a couch. The average dining room derived its name—*triclinium*—because it accommodated three couches. A wealthy household would have several such rooms. Frequently, the meal was accompanied or followed by entertainment including music, dancing, acrobatics or readings. After dark, oil lamps on tall bronze stands illuminated the rooms. The walls would have been painted, possibly creating an illusion of depth and, in the latest style, presenting fantasy architecture or the illusion of a naturalistic landscape with figures. Possibly in Herodes and Annia's house there would be scenes with religious or philosophical meaning which could be discussed. There would be a library. Sculpture would abound—classical originals or skilful replicas produced in the numerous Greek workshops. On the tables silverware gleamed.

Annia's taste would be reflected in her Athenian home, and due to the instant embalming of Pompeii, only some sixty years previously, we have been able to see what these interiors might have been like. And Pompeii came to London's Royal Academy for three months in 1977 when a unique exhibition from the Museo Archeologico Nazionale in Naples occupied their galleries. Its Academic Advisor was Ward Perkins.

Annia Regilla gave birth to four more children while she lived in Greece. After Elpinice, the next child was also a girl, but then she produced a male heir, who was named Bradua but who, apparently, had learning difficulties and was a disappointment to his father. Then there was another son, Regillus, who, however, did not reach maturity. In bearing children, Annia, would have the best gynaecologists available, for they were recognised to be Greek. In running her large households she would have had plenty of help including the servants and companions she had brought with her. She could have had a leisurely time, reclined in a saffron robe after bathing daily in asses milk had she wished, but Annia Regilla, as the evidence shows, led a demanding public life. She became a priestess.

XVI

ANNIA AS PRIESTESS

The climate of the time was favourable for priestesses. Even in the early Christian movement women held important positions. It was to be centuries before a predominantly male convocation pronounced all women as unfit to hold priestly office. By that time Christianity had become the official religion of the Roman Empire, but in its early years the assemblies of Christians which preceded the establishment of churches were sometimes presided over by women. They were the bishops of their flocks and all members seem to have been considered equal despite differences in ethnic or social background and regardless of gender. There is a second century fresco in the catacombs of Pricilla in Rome showing women presiding over the Eucharist.

Regilla's family was unlikely to be aware of these activities which were carried out in secret, but the highest power in the land, Rome's first emperor Augustus (27 BC-14 AD), had supported the revival of women-oriented cults. Rich women from aristocratic families such as Regilla's, who could support the considerable expenses of the cult were appointed as priestesses.

This continued under Emperor Hadrian (48-117 AD) who had a special interest in things of the spirit with a particular leaning towards Greek culture. As a child he had so enthusiastically embraced his Greek studies that he had earned for himself the racially slanted nickname of Graeculus, 'little Greek boy', and his philhellenism only deepened with time. A contemporary historian described him as being 'excessively keen on poetry and literature'. He was also skilled in painting and enjoyed music as a singer and a player of the *kithara*. He did not, however, find the official Roman religion satisfying. It was not intended to be so but concentrated on complicated rituals at home and in public to secure the favour of the gods. The Greek cults, on the other hand, offered mysticism and ecstatic experiences to the initiated. It was this that appealed to Hadrian. His visits to Greece throughout his life were frequent and culminated in his initiation into the mysteries of the Eleusinian cult founded on the myth of Demeter.

In such a favourable atmosphere as this it was possible that Annia Regilla would have become a priestess even if she had remained in Rome. It is certain, however, that by marrying Herodes and eventually moving with him to Greece she found the greatest opportunities for the expression of her talents in the position of priestess.

Herodes had given Athens a fine stadium, which was a transformation of the original one into a more flexible arena where all sorts of competitions would be held. It was completed in 143/44 when Annia and Herodes arrived in Greece, and soon afterwards Herodes inaugurated a new cult with Annia Regilla serving as its first priestess. This, of course, was something that Herodes, as provider of the fine building, was uniquely able to do. He and Annia may well have discussed and planned it for some time. The new cult, appropriately, was that of Tyche, goddess of fortune. Competitive events took place in this stadium more frequently than anywhere else in the Greek world, attracting competitors and spectators from many other cities. They included oratorical contests in which Herodes would take part as well as performing introductory and funerary orations. It is likely that ceremonies relating to Tyche, goddess of fortune, would be held in connection with all these events. Annia would be frequently involved and as the first priestess in a new cult there would be much to work out, but with an experienced philosopher/teacher husband and experts to call upon young Annia would get the help she needed.

A temple for the goddess was built by Herodes high on a hill above the rows of seating at one side of the stadium. Of white marble, with surrounding columns in the Ionic style, the temple contained a statue of the goddess carved in ivory. Annia would ascend a monumental flight of steps to this high point and her progress, with musical accompaniment, can be imagined as part of the ceremony. Her position was, in every sense, a high one. As a young woman of barely twenty she could reflect upon it with some wonder—elevated above an audience which could number over 50,000, as in the Colosseum.

The Athens stadium was also a centre where famous Sophists, among them Herodes, would hold philosophical discussions. Herodes and Annia would be frequently appearing—the outstanding partnership of the time. It is not therefore surprising that Herodes would be brought by the citizens of Athens from his estate in Marathon, where he planned to be buried, to a tomb on the opposite side of the stadium to the temple of Tyche. The significance of this placing opposite the temple of his priestess partner is inescapable.

The second cult for which Annia was to be appointed priestess was at Olympia, the home of the ancient Games. This cult was not a new one, as at Athens, but centuries old. The main place for its celebration was at Eleusis where, as we know, Emperor Hadrian had gone to be initiated into its mysteries. Annia, therefore, would have needed, and would have received, expert guidance in the rituals of the ancient cult. The sanctuary of the goddess was at the bottom of a low hill on the north side of the race course. The marble altar where sacrifices were made was across from the judges viewing stand—a prime location close to events. As the priestess of Demeter Annia Regilla was the only woman allowed to be present at the Olympics, where the athletes competed naked. The slaves who attended on the priestess would be male. In Rome the athletes did not exercise nude, only in the Colosseum might Annia have seen naked men in contests but it is not likely that a young teenager from an aristocratic family would have been allowed to attend these often bloodthirsty spectacles. They were certainly not to the tastes of the Greeks who avoided violent shows and preferred to see their dramas in the theatre.

The myth of Demeter on which the cult was based celebrated the yearly rebirth of growing things and also gave the promise of afterlife. The story goes that goddess Demeter's beautiful daughter, Persephone, was abducted by Zeus' brother Hades, lord of the underworld, and whisked off to his realm. Demeter had no idea where she was and began a long search. When, however, the grieving mother did eventually learn of her whereabouts she was shocked to learn that Zeus had actually connived in the abduction by his brother. In her anger at the gods who had allowed this to happen Demeter made the earth barren and unfruitful. Lack of corn resulted in famine and eventually Zeus was forced to fetch Persephone back to earth. Unfortunately Hades had secretly given her a pomegranate to eat and, since she had eaten while in the underworld, she could not leave it completely but had to spend four months of each year as the wife of Hades. Demeter, once joyfully united with her daughter, accepted this and made the earth give rich harvests again after four dormant months.

The story gave Annia plenty of opportunities for the expression of Demeter's feelings; patient love, trust, anger, courage, feminine strength and ultimately joy. It had many aspects. The return from the underworld was a type of resurrection. The struggle with the gods was even a precursor of the feminist struggle for women's rights.

And there was surely scope for Annia to use music, for it was believed that music made the gods more approachable. This was particularly so in Greece, as we learn from Nero, one of the worst of emperors but an outstanding lover of poetry and the arts. He took part in many literary and dramatic contests in Greece and remarked: 'The Greeks are worthy of my efforts; they really listen to music.'

How strongly Annia and Herodes themselves believed in the reality of the governing influence of this quarrelsome family of gods we can only speculate. It is certainly something they would discuss. Belief in the gods was beginning to fade and in the next century Christianity would officially become the religion of the Roman Empire. Herodes, as we know, was an independent thinker ready to question the conventional belief of the Stoics and act differently. He may well, as a philosopher, have been aware of what a certain Christian disciple, within sight of the Parthenon, had said about an altar to an unknown god?

In the public performance of her office, however, Annia Regilla would take no chances. Many would believe that good harvests depended on it. Indeed, she was so effective and appreciated as a priestess that she herself, as we shall later see, became closely identified with a goddess.

In return for the honour of being appointed priestess of the cult at Olympia, Annia and Herodes financed several works there, the most impressive and useful of which is a *nymphaeum* or fountain. Olympia was a hot and dusty place, especially in the height of summer when the Games were held. Annia, no doubt remembering her own experience on the journey to Athens when they had arrived at her family's estate in southern Italy and found insufficient water available to give her little daughter a decent wash, knew the importance of a clean and plentiful supply for athletes, attendants and visitors.

As before in Italy, this was a joint project; Herodes built the aqueduct bringing the water, and Annia the fountain with its statuary. Although subsequent scholars have attributed the whole construction to Herodes, a surviving inscription incised on the base of a statue of a bull representing the top god Zeus leaves no doubt in the matter. It reads 'Regilla, priestess of Demeter, dedicated the water and the things connected with the water to Zeus.'

Financed by her own wealth, Annia Regilla's nymphaeum was a very impressive monument as can be reconstructed from the extent of the foundations and the surviving statuary. Behind the fountain pool itself rose two tiers of figures. Sculptures were either free-standing or in niches, and the central niche, at each level, was occupied by a statue of Zeus. At the lower level were statues of the imperial family to whom, of course, Annia was related, and at the upper level were portrait statues of Herodes and Annia's own family. Immediately left of Zeus was Annia herself and next to her both her parents, her grandfather and her daughter Elpinice. To the right of Zeus stood Herodes, his parents, his son Bradua, and the two youngest children, Athenais and Regillus. Unfortunately, most of the surviving statues, including that of Herodes, are headless. Annia's head has become detached from its statue and is so damaged that nothing of her features can be made out. Her draped figure, however, shows that she wears the same dress as the women in the imperial Roman family and is tall and well proportioned. In fact, she appears to be of slimmer build than her daughter Elpinice.

The predominantly Roman character of the statuary, the portayals of the Roman imperial family, including Emperor Hadrian and the emperor-to-be Marcus Aurelius, together with her own family would mean that Annia Regilla could feel very much at home with her monumental fountain. We can imagine the joyful inauguration ceremonies of this superbly useful gift.

Annia Regilla had become a major presence in Greek cultural life and could surely reflect with satisfaction on the way things had worked out for her following the marriage to Herodes. But her fame spread wider than Athens and Olympia. At the important town of Corinth, although she did not hold priestly office, she was held to be the practically a personification of the goddess Tyche. A statue was erected in her honour and the surviving marble base bears this dedication:

> This is a portrait of Regilla. A sculptor carved the figure endowing the stone with all her self-control *(sophrosyne)*. The great Herodes Atticus, outstanding beyond others for attaining the pinnacle of every virtue, gave it. She chose as her husband, acclaimed among all the Greeks, a descendant and flower of Archaea, surpassing all. Regilla, the Council, as if calling you 'Tyche' has erected this marble image in front of the sanctuary.

The description says that the sculptor worked from the live model which makes it all the more regrettable that only the lower half of the statue together with its dedication survives. The very flattering nature of the inscription also reflects the gratitude of the citizens of Corinth for several major works there funded by Herodes and Annia, but the archaeological evidence is confused. Regilla may have financed the renovation of a fountain complex, as at Olympia. It portrays Regilla's family and the imperial family, as does another fountain at Priene nearby. All surviving female statues are, however, headless and have been removed from their original sites.

A base from a statue dedicated to her found near the Priene fountain is particularly interesting. It has carved on it a garland surrounding three musical instruments. This indicates Regilla's musical talents, and her cultivation of the art, and subsequently Herodes was to build and dedicate an *odeion*, or musical theatre, to her. The brief inscription on the base again refers to her *sophrosyne* or 'self-control', a quality traditionally praised in Greek women and which must have been clearly displayed by the Roman Regilla. It reads:

> As commanded by the Council of Sisyphus, by the streams of the fountains you see me, Regilla, the image of *sophrosyne*.

Unfortunately we do not 'see' her as no portrait head survives from all the statues dedicated to her. There are even dedications including her at Delphi. Clearly, Annia Regilla was famous and highly, even affectionately, regarded as a priestess and philanthropist in her time and in her own right, not completely overshadowed by her Greek husband as the mists of time and wrongful attributions have made her.

Despite these many activities the couple would have had time to spend on Herodes extensive estate at Marathon just to the east of Athens. Following his marriage Herodes gave a significant area of it to Annia Regilla, marking the distinction with a large and imposing gateway in part of a three-mile wall surrounding her property. According to classical scholars no other example of such a separation of adjacent estates belonging to this period has been found, and was contrary to the contemporary ideas of marital property which was to be held in common according to the Stoics and others. As we have already seen, however, Herodes, did not feel he should act as others thought he should. On one side of the gate was inscribed:

>the place you enter belongs to Regilla

and on the other:

>the place you enter belongs to Herodes

Popularly known as the 'Gate of eternal Harmony' it was given an even more resounding title in the Guide to Greece which the Greek travel writer Pausanias wrote in the second century for Roman and Greek tourists. Here it is given the title 'Gate of Immortal Unanimity'.

The partnership of Herodes and Annia was clearly unique, one which they publicly celebrated and which, while being essentially co-operative, had space within it for each to pursue their own interests. What Annia Regilla did in her space we can only speculate as no architectural remains have been found. The terrain is barren and desolate now but in classical times it would have been quite different. The area around the Bay of Marathon attracted throngs of Athenians each year to celebrate their famous victory and the estates of Herodes and Annia would have been kept by hundreds of slaves in whatever style their owners wished. We can be sure there would have been no lack of water to cultivate groves or gardens. Did Annia use hers to rehearse the music, choral and instrumental, for her priestess events, as well as for her other activities with children, friends and visitors? She would have the freedom and means to do all of this.

Their partnership in Greece had been richly creative. Annia Regilla had become renowned as a priestess, Herodes had continued to speak as 'the voice of Athens' with his orations; both had been responsible for creating useful and even magnificent monuments in famous cities. They were the equivalent of present day celebrities and, as such, would have numerous fans and, no doubt, some enemies.

What more they might have achieved together we shall never know since Annia's sixth pregnancy ended fatally.

XVII
HERODES ON TRIAL

It would be sometime before the news of Annia Regilla's death reached Rome, and then her brother Bradua, who was now head of the Appia family since her father had died, decided to bring a murder charge against Herodes. The charge is quoted by historian Philostratus as follows: 'When his wife Regilla was eight months pregnant he ordered his freedman Alcimedon to beat her for trivial reasons. She died in premature childbirth from a blow to her abdomen.' This accusation which must have originated in Athens is not ascribed to any person or persons. Bradua, at the trial, never referred to any witnesses nor produced any evidence to support it. The charge simply rests on this statement which is essentially anonymous.

The Roman judicial system was wide open to abuse, for there was no police force or prosecution procedure as we know it. Accusations could be made by virtually anybody who could gain a hearing. Emperor Hadrian had been much troubled by advocates who specialised in bringing charges on fabricated evidence in order to discredit the accused and have their property confiscated. He therefore sought to improve matters by forbidding anonymous accusations. Because of the standing of the Appia family in Rome and his own position as a consul, Bradua ensured the charge, although it was essentially anonymous, would gain a hearing. There is, incidentally, no record of Bradua having visited his sister in Greece or being interested in her. It was a question of family honour.

At such a trial there were just two speakers: the accuser and the defendant, who could speak either for themselves of hire lawyers to do so. Naturally Bradua and Herodes spoke for themselves. The trial would be held before a large jury of Roman senators, perhaps fifty or so, and the proceedings were conducted in Latin.

Bradua simply used his time to deliver an oration about himself and the status of his family. There are no reports of any evidence being produced or even referred to by him or anybody else. For Herodes, appearing in Rome so soon after his wife's death, it must have been a truly traumatic experience. He had to speak, not in his own native tongue but in no doubt fluent

Latin, and before a jury, who, we may reasonably assume, were partly hostile. Annia Regilla's family were Roman aristocracy. Herodes, as far as we know, had been absent from Rome for some fifteen years and it was Greece, not Rome that had benefited from his activities. The jury, no doubt, included some who had been offended by his outspokenness and sometime arrogant behaviour. He would have wished to praise Annia Regilla's qualities and expand on their partnership activities—she as priestess and philanthropist, a builder of useful monuments—but would his listeners have seen or even heard of that? He was grieving for her death but stood accused of having been the cause of it!

In Philostatus' account of the trial Herodes denied giving any order to Alcimedon to punish his wife and stated that, when he returned and questioned the household he had been informed that she had spontaneously and fatally miscarried. What motive could he possibly have had in bringing about his wife's death while pregnant with his child? Herodes was acquitted and no one was punished. The Senate's judgement was without appeal.

Since then, however, it has been suggested that Herodes was guilty and the trial was a miscarriage of justice. The latest example is the 2007 book with the title *The Murder of Regilla. A Case of Domestic Violence in Antiquity* by Sarah B Pomeroy. In order to re-open a trial one would expect there to be new evidence. There is none, only re-interpretation, speculation and suggestion which a defending lawyer, had there been one, would be able to question as I propose to do. The suggestion, for instance, that there was a constant cause for friction within such a racially divided marriage. On the contrary there is evidence of full understanding and co-operation between the Greek and Roman couple who lived so much of their lives in public and surrounded by friends and servants. Annia was appreciated, not isolated, in her husband's country. It is no secret that Herodes was an emotional man and sometimes unable or unwilling to control anger. His construction activities, as every architect knows, give rise occasionally to frustration, but that his wife should give him cause for anger is unimaginable. Annia Regilla was, on the contrary, the perfect wife for him and with her renowned *sophrosyne* ('self-control') could have a soothing calming influence.

They had children, including a boy, Bradua, with learning difficulties, who gave great concern to his father. It is possible that Annia and Herodes had different opinions about the way he should be brought up. Herodes would be more severe; Annia, more lenient, possibly appearing to spoil the child, and this could cause argument, though hardly punishment.

How, then, can the origin of the charge be explained? Herodes is known to have had many enemies in Athens, even dating back to the days of his inheritance. Just how determined these enemies were can be seen fifteen years later at Sirmium when they conspired to accuse him of acting treasonably against the emperor himself—a charge as dramatic and unlikely as the one of murdering his wife—

which will be considered in the next chapter. In fact, the lurid accusation of a 'kick to the abdomen of a wife in the final month of her pregnancy' reads like a sensational line in a tabloid newspaper. Perhaps the Athenians felt that they could feed it to a jealous and possibly hellenophobic brother-in-law and embarrass Herodes?

At this distance how can we presume to know better than the jury that acquitted Herodes? Yet in the recent book it is stated: 'Bradua's accusation is so specific that we may assume that Herodes was acquitted only because he was protected by Marcus Aurelius.' We already know that they were friends. But we have seen in an earlier chapter concerning an earlier trial that Marcus Aurelius was quite clear that Herodes should *not* be given special treatment. Moreover, it is doubtful whether Marcus Aurelius was even emperor at the time of the trial which took place sometime in early 161. In March of that year the previous emperor Antoninus Pius died and Marcus succeeded him jointly with the younger Lucius Verus. Whoever was emperor we can imagine them to be too busy to be directly concerned in influencing a senatorial jury. In his tribute to Pius, moreover, Marcus praises the fact that 'he never listened to slander' and he himself would never do so. Marcus Aurelius is the least likely of all emperors, as we can tell from his *Meditations* and his behaviour, to be swayed by personal feelings and to allow a 'miscarriage of justice' to occur.

What were the circumstances of Regilla's death? She was in her late thirties and childbearing until forty was considered normal. She would have had the best attention, but still there were conditions that could occur in advanced pregnancy and life expectancy for even upper class women was not high. Marcus' wife, Faustina, having born at least fourteen children, was forty-five years old when she died during a pregnancy. In more recent times one of Queen Victoria's children died suddenly and inexplicably during pregnancy and her doctor subsequently committed suicide out of remorse.

Philostratus details the age of the foetus as 'of eight months gestation', because this could supply a reason for its death. Greek and Roman medical writers believed that a baby born at eight months would not live and that giving birth to such a baby would be fatal to the mother. It was believed to be unlucky probably with some evidence.

Despite the outcome of the trial and the complete dismissal of the accusation, what the grieving Herodes did afterwards has been used to interpret his state of mind and to judge his guilt or innocence, so we shall now consider this.

XVIII

HERODES' TRIBUTES TO ANNIA

One of the first things Herodes did after Regilla's death was to add these lines to the inscription on the Gate of Harmony at their estate in Marathon:

> Blessed is the person who has built a new city,
> giving it the name 'Regilla's' he lives exulting,
> but I live grieving that this estate exists for me
> without my dear wife and my home is half complete.
> Thus the gods mix a lifetime for mortals
> having both joys and sorrows as neighbours.

Pomeroy finds this 'lugubrious' and 'maudlin'. I find it poignant, brief, and a natural expression from a grieving husband. A loving husband; note the reference of 'joys' of their time together.

But the first lines are particularly interesting in their reference to building a city named after the beloved. This is something only emperors could do, not even Herodes with his massive wealth, and the emperor he has in mind is Hadrian. They had met. They were both constructors and interested in beautifying Athens; Hadrian even travelled with a team of building specialists, and Hadrian is famous for building a city in memory of the young Antinous who had drowned, mysteriously, in the Nile some thirty years previously while they were on their travels. Within a week the emperor decided to found a new city to be called Antinoopolis opposite the place where his beloved had been found. The city was splendid, arranged in a grid with its two main streets crossing at the city centre where a shrine was dedicated to a new divinity Antinous. Statues of him abound in antiquity. It was one of the great love stories of the time. Many of the new town's buildings were, apparently intact three centuries ago, but almost nothing remains today thanks to the depredations of local people. Which depredations continue, for as I write I have before me a *Christian Science Monitor* report of regular looting 'of the ancient Roman city of Antinoopolis … due to the lack of security since the uprising in Egypt 2011'. It is ironic to think that the greatest memorial to a loved one that Herodes could envisage, and wish to emulate, should prove so transient.

More fortunate is the fate of the *odeion*, or recital hall, which Herodes build to commemorate Regilla. Constructed in less than fourteen years and finished by 174 AD it still graces the south slope of the Acropolis below the Parthenon. It was the largest *odeion* in Greece and held an audience of 5,000. The seats, pavement and walls were covered with white marble and a remarkably engineered cedar roof spanned the space giving it excellent acoustics. The musical and theatrical arts were traditionally sacred to Dionysus and Apollo so it had, like Regilla, divine associations. A more appropriate memorial to her memory and musical talents cannot be imagined. There is nothing unnatural about it or suggestive of the product of a guilty conscience. Extravagant it may be, but surely entirely suitable? A touching aspect, to which Pomeroy draws attention, is that it is built like a Roman theatre, in contrast to the neighbouring theatre of Dionysus and Herodes' Panathenaic stadium: a tribute to Annia Regilla's Roman origins.

About this time, during the construction of the Odeion, perhaps when it was nearing completion, we have a vivid glimpse of Herodes, in the report of an incident which took place at Sirmium, where Emperor Marcus Aurelius had his headquarters during a war. Apparently Marcus carried on his judicial business as uninterrupted as possible. 'Whenever he had spare time from the war he held court.'

One of the cases involved his friend and former tutor, Herodes Atticus, and it is reported in some detail by Philostratus in his *Lives of the Sophists* and quoted in Birley's biography of Marcus as follows: 'it had its origin in the hostility shown to Herodes by the Quintilii brothers of Latin origin … who had been acting as special commissioners in the province. Herodes disliked these two brothers and indulged in the luxury of calling them "Trojans", which for a Greek may have been a pleasant joke [my English mock serious jokes were often taken seriously in Sweden and I had to stop using them]. The Quintilii, however, reacted, encouraged Herodes' enemies, and hostility towards him in Athens grew.'

Herodes brought a charge of 'conspiracy to set the people against him' before the proconsul, and his adversaries appealed to Marcus, hoping to find him favourable to their side, Philostratus says, because Marcus suspected Herodes of having intrigued treasonably with his co-emperor Lucius against him (an unlikely assertion, but his enemies made it).

Herodes brought with him to Sirmium twin girls whom he had looked after from childhood. They were the daughters of his freedman Alcimedon (the same who had been accused by Bradua of delivering a blow which reputedly brought about Annia's fatal miscarriage). These twins had been born about the same time and were now young teenagers. These girls would have been playmates for Annia's child had it survived. Herodes never had any grandchildren and he was, apparently, very attached to the two and made them his cupbearers and cooks.

Shortly before the tribunal met these twin girls were killed by lightning while they were asleep in the tower where Herodes and his party were lodging in the suburbs of the town. Herodes, apparently, was driven frantic with grief at this tragedy, and when he appeared before the emperor all his usual eloquence deserted him. Instead, he attacked Marcus violently: 'This is all I get in return for my hospitality to Lucius—though it was you who sent him to me!'

The prefect in charge thought that in speaking out like this against the emperor only one conclusion was possible: Herodes obviously wanted to die. Herodes replied: 'My good fellow an old man fears little' and swept out of the court before his allotted time was up.

Marcus 'did not frown or change his expression' but told the other side to make their defence 'even though Herodes does not give you leave.'

Marcus listened for some time without showing his feelings, but eventually the whole attack on Herodes moved him to open tears. However, the attack was not only on Herodes personally, but also on his freedmen. These Marcus punished, although mildly, and Alcimedon was pardoned on the grounds that the loss of his daughters had already caused him sufficient suffering. It is probable that Marcus advised Herodes to live away from Athens for a time.

Here we see the two friends face to face; Herodes at his most emotional and losing his eloquence; the normally controlled emperor crying in public! We see Herodes making trouble for himself by first creating enemies, and then taking them to court where they will attempt to cause him maximum harm, even slandering him with a charge as sensational as murdering his wife; plotting treason against the emperor! No wonder Herodes, bereft of Annia Regilla's moderating influence and under emotional stress, goes to pieces and truly endangers his own life.

Marcus Aurelius, however, was a peacemaker, a kind-hearted man, always wishing to bring harmony to relationships, especially between his friends. In this case he is visibly moved, which must have been rare, but patiently listens and punishes where he sees necessary but then does the best he can to repair the damage. Following the hearing he had a great marble plaque inscribed with the rulings on a series of matters including those involving Herodes and adds his personal hope that 'Herodes, with his famous enthusiasm for education should in future, together with the Athenians, share the enjoyment of their festivals, both religious and secular. Since the causes of conflict were removed would it not be possible for them to love my Herodes, who is also their Herodes?'

Their friendship was to continue until the death of Herodes round about 177. According to Philostratus he left instructions to be buried at his Marathon estate, but the Athenians eventually buried him at the Panathenaic stadium he built, just across from the temple of Tyche where

Regilla had been priestess. Where she is buried or was cremated is not known with any certainty, but Pomeroy refers to an inscription which was found in Rome in the gardens of Palatine, taken to England, described and published in 1676, but subsequently lost. It refers to a monument dedicated to Regilla and must have been at the building on the Appia estate which we are now to consider.

The inscription reads in part:

> Herodes dedicated this monument also to commemorate his misfortune and his wife's virtue.
> But this is not a burial. Her body is in Greece and now beside her husband.

This indicates that the building Herodes raised for Annia Regilla on the Appia estate never contained her body. Although similar to the second century tombs I had seen beneath St Peter's, it is more accurately referred to as a cenotaph.

'The Cenotaph of Annia Regilla' is therefore the correct title for the building which I first saw in the winter of 1953 referred to in my guidebook as 'Tempio del Dio Redicolo', being used as an outhouse by the adjoining farm. Its beauty, as I could see even in its partly ruined state, made me decide to devote my time in Rome to measuring it in order to produce a drawn restoration in colour of its original appearance.

I knew nothing at the time of its creator but in the sixty years since then the story of Annia Regilla and Herodes Atticus has gradually unfolded for me. I now see their partnership as an outstanding example of the fusion of Greek and Roman cultures; a fusion which has been of tremendous significance in world history.

The cenotaph is the most intimate of the memorials Herodes erected to Annia after her death, and the one which has best survived to indicate Herodes' thoughts and feelings and now shapes the final chapter of their story.

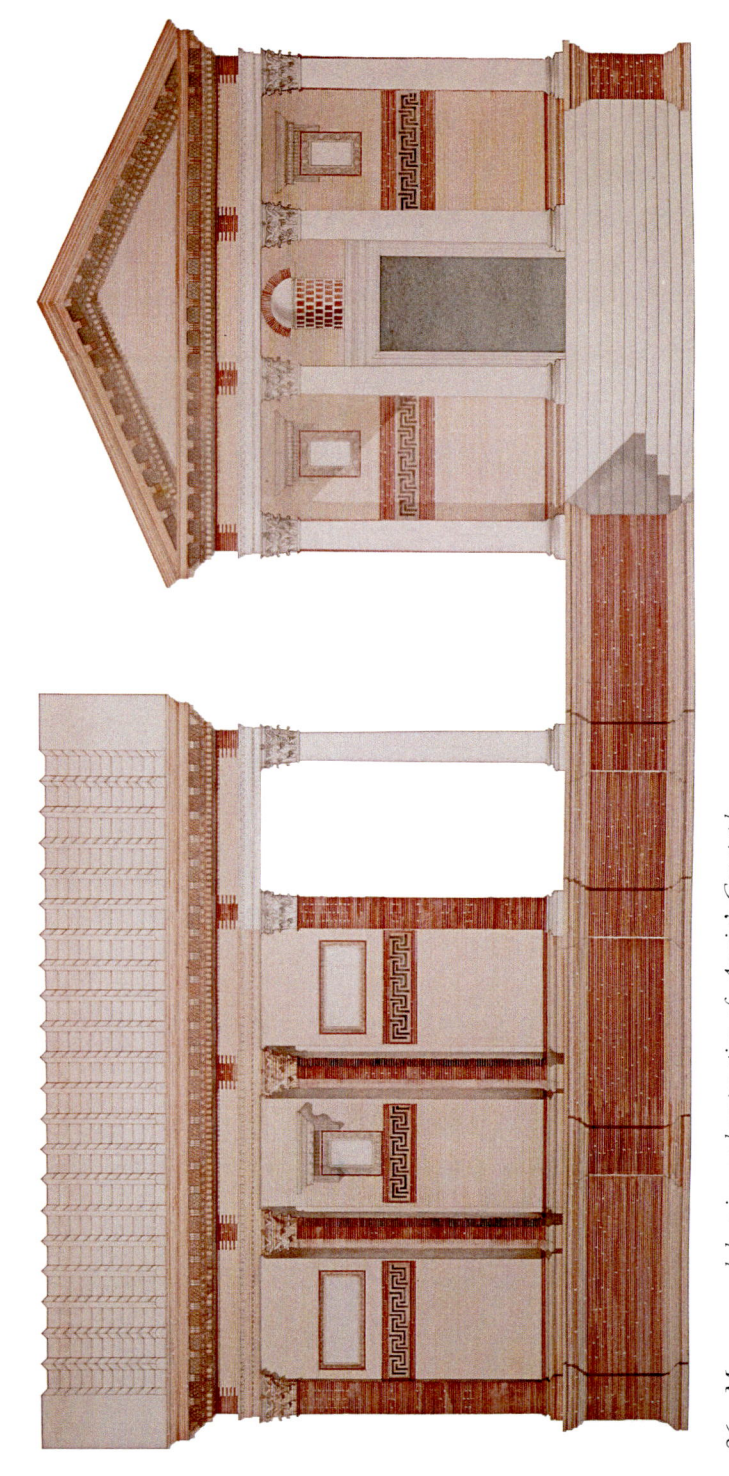

26 *My measured drawing and restoration of Annia's Cenotaph, north and east sides.*

XIX

THE CENOTAPH

Far from being an extravagant public display of grief, Annia Regilla's cenotaph is a building of modest size, erected on a private family estate outside the walls of Rome. It was intended to be a place of private reflection for friends and family. Herodes could not have known that its location was to prove a blessing. Relatively remote, wrongly attributed and given little attention, it has survived out in the Campagna, an area not subject, like central Rome, to the pressures of redevelopment.

The building you see today retains much of its original appearance, and in my measured restoration I have restored the missing parts. At first sight how Roman it looks despite being built by a Greek! The materials of which it is constructed, brick and terracotta-faced concrete, are typically Roman, although used with outstanding finesse and bravura. Its appearance is completely in harmony with its Roman environment, yet the Greek origin of its creator is unmistakably announced by the prominent Greek key motif laid in black pumice stone in the frieze at mid-height which runs round all sides encircling the building. Like an embrace.

Everything to do with the design would have been a personal decision by Herodes. There were no imposed requirements and no limitations. Two possible models he might have had in mind, however, were a Grecian temple and a Roman house-tomb of the time. Like the temple it is intended to be seen from all sides and, like a temple, it is raised on a podium and would have been approached by a flight of steps. Columns would have surrounded a temple. In his brick-faced building Herodes has divided the external walls into panels by adding full height pilasters in brickwork of a contrasting colour. Thus, like a peristyle, there is a regular rhythm around the building which continues in the marble columns of the entrance portico in my restoration.

A temple has a completely symmetrical exterior. Herodes, however, departs from this model in an original way. As the approach road to the estate is from the Via Caffarella on the east it is this side of the building which visitors would first pass. Wishing to make it more interesting and beautiful, Herodes transforms the two central pilasters into apparently octagonal columns set

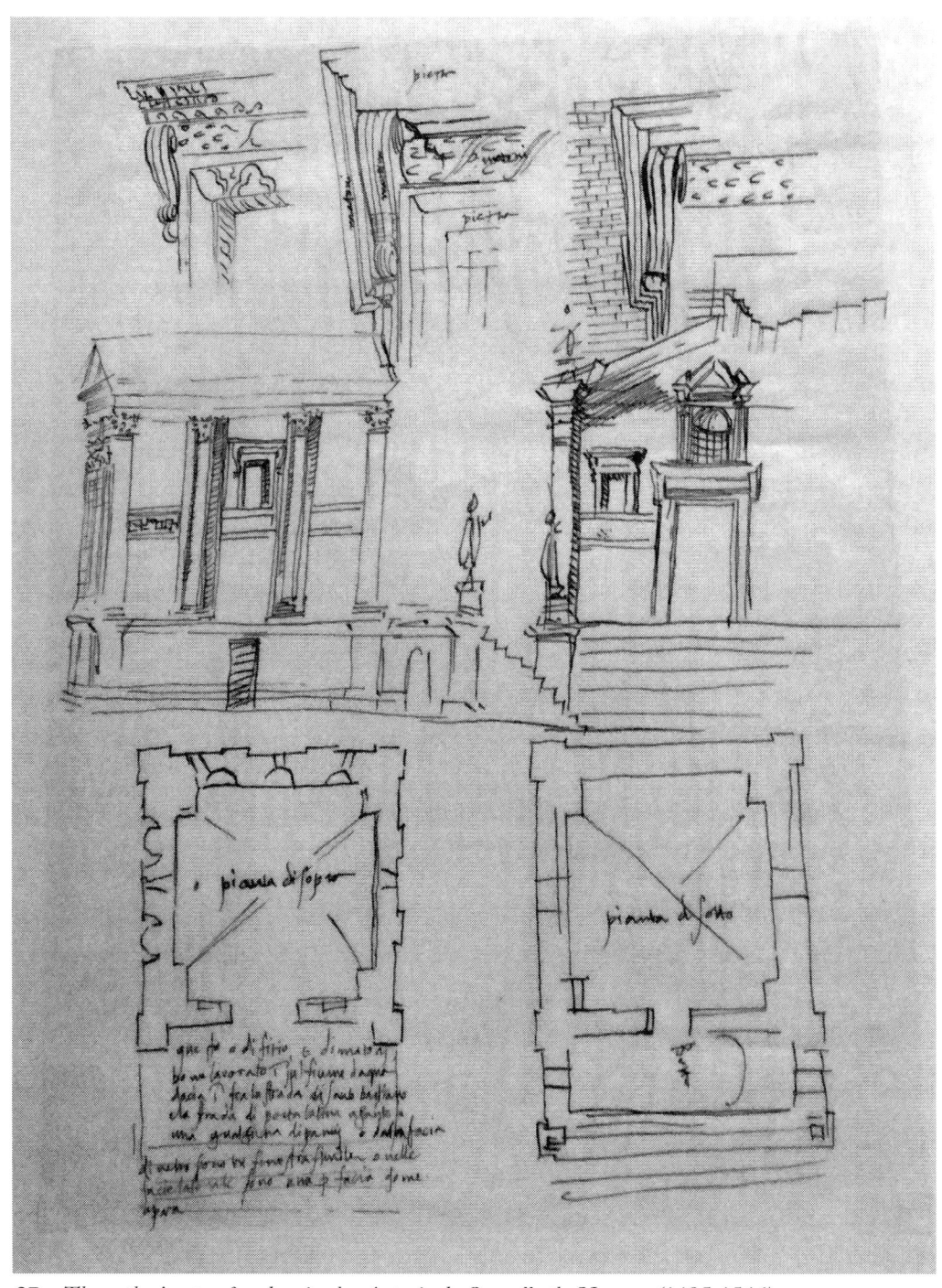

27   The author's copy of a drawing by Antonio da Sangallo the Younger (1485-1546)

in semi-circular recesses. This is Roman brickwork at its most virtuosic produced by the finest craftsmen in the service of a rich and exacting employer. It was this feature which fascinated Renaissance architects, including Antonio da Sangallo the Younger, whose sketches I found in the British School Library. Herodes, using Roman brickwork to suggest detached columns, has devised something quite remarkable!

As we can see, the vertical pilasters and the horizontal frieze divide the external walls into a series of panels which unify the building. They are all squares. The square, being non-directional, gives a sense of repose and timelessness to a building. This proportion relates all the facades, and the body of the building itself forms a cube. All fine building has this unity or governing idea, and in the School's Library I had found a small book, a translation of *Plotinus on the Beautiful*, which, although from a few decades later, indicates the unifying thought process which a philosopher such as Herodes may have had:

> Where the Forming-idea has entered, it has grouped and coordinated what from a diversity of parts was to become a unity, it has wrought the diversity to a determined reality, stamping on it the unity of harmonious coherence; for the idea is a unity and what it shapes must become a unity in the degree possible to what is formed from diversity. And on what has thus been brought into unity, Beauty enthrones itself, giving itself to the parts as to the sum; when it lights on a natural unity indistinguishable into parts then it gives itself to that whole ... .

There is a special place for sculpture on the building. Although Sangallo in his sketch suggests a statue at the top of the steps, this is his fancy, an echo of numerous statues which adorned the Italian villas of his time. The place for sculpture on this building is the niche prepared for it in the portico, directly above the entrance door. The vertical proportion of this niche shows that it was intended for a single figure. It would have contained the image of Annia Regilla.

In wondering about the figure which Herodes, newly widowed, would have commissioned for this niche, I thought of a Swedish phrase for the recently deceased, that they 'go out of time'. Unfamiliar to English ears it is a simple truth, which also applies in a degree, to those left behind, for, as a widower, I found my most vivid images of Britt ranged freely in time and were often from our early years together. I think it is quite likely that Herodes would want an image of Annia as a vibrant young woman for this niche, and I found such an image illustrated in Donald Strong's brilliantly clear book on *The Classical World*. It is a small bronze statuette in the British Museum, of Italian workmanship, imitating the archaic sculpture of Greece and has a lively presence and forward movement. In the absence of any surviving portrait of Annia Regilla, I suggest it as a possible focus for thoughts about this statue.

28   This small bronze statuette in the British Museum is the sort of vibrant image of Annia which Herodes could well have commissioned for the niche above the entrance to her cenotaph. It was made in the Roman period but imitates the style of archaic Greek figures of the sixth century BC and was acquired by the museum in 1873 from a famous Italian jeweller and antiques collector who probably set the diamonds in her eyes and inlaid with silver the Greek key pattern which can be seen along the edge of her dress.
It is this pattern which Herodes put all round the building, like an embrace, to proclaim its Greek origin. In the same way this pattern on the dress could be said to proclaim Annia's partnership with Herodes, and what could be more appropriate? Photograph courtesy of the British Museum.

Then there are the windows to be considered. These, in their elegantly detailed surrounds, occur on all four walls and the largest number on the south-facing wall. The house-tombs in a Roman necropolis are not provided with windows like this. The explanation must be that Herodes wished to have plenty of daylight to illuminate the interior. (Window glass was already being used in the later buildings of Pompeii and would have been used here.) Why the day-lighting? We should remember that this was not a tomb. The interiors I had seen under St Peter's had square or semi-circular niches in their walls to receive urns with ashes or, as inhumation gradually superseded cremation during the second and third centuries, places for sarcophagi. But, as we know, Herodes and Annia were laid to rest in Athens as their children would have been. This building, therefore, did not function as a family tomb but rather as a temple to the memory of Annia Regilla. Its interior would have contained statues depicting her as a priestess to Demeter and Tyche, together with paintings, mosaic and stucco evocations of her life. It would have been colourful and, above all, as beautiful as the best artists working for Herodes could make it. Such art needs light to be properly seen and Herodes placed the windows to provide it in generous measure.

Such lighting would also enable Herodes to experience and to share the interior with friends and visitors at any time during the day or evening. Ceremonial meals might take place on anniversaries or feast days and we can imagine Herodes spending hours in and around his building. Herodes outlived Annia by some sixteen years and only died in his late seventies (confounding the contemporary statistics for longevity). It would be wrong, however, to think of these years as a widower as 'declining years' remembering his own critical words on the Stoic view which he saw as 'to rule out the more active emotions of the spirit and grow old in torpor, a sluggish enervated life'.

He would probably divide his time between Italy and Greece, his wife's country and his own, as I do. In Athens he would oversee the completion of the *odeion*, participating in events at this music theatre, especially those commemorating Annia. He would continue his teaching and hospitality to friends and students. Then, before the heat of the summer arrived, travelling north to this estate in the Campagna to enjoy its more temperate climate and its fruitfulness.

Herodes would, no doubt, add to the contents of Annia Regilla's Cenotaph from time to time, and he would need to ensure that the perfect finish of the exterior was maintained for, extraordinary as it may seem, in addition to the various colours of brickwork and terracotta, it was also painted. While measuring, I came across, and still have, a fragment of the paint, and each brick joint would have been lined in white. The building must have gleamed in the sun like an enamelled jewel and enchanted invited friends and visitors.

Brother-in-law Bradua, however, is not likely to have been among them. We do not know what became of him. He disappears from the historical record following the trial. Nothing is known of any continuation of his political career or of any marriage.

Among friends who would, however, have a part in Herodes' life we know that the relationship with Marcus Aurelius endured. Such a long and unbroken friendship between two men of such different character and belief is remarkable and must tell us something. Not that it was a friendship based on the receipt of favours, as some have thought, for Marcus' high code of behaviour excluded the giving of favours, and it was beneath Herodes to ask for them or to act in a subservient way, as we have seen from his conduct at Sirmium. It must have been a friendship based on respect for each other's way of thinking and a true affection.

We do have an image of Herodes during these years as a widower. Found on his estate at Marathon, this marble bust is now in the Louvre where I saw it in 1979 and noted that it showed a 'serious, thoughtful and handsome man'. The biographer Graindor describes it in more detail: 'His hair is thick and curly, descending over a broad and lined forehead. The eyes are large and dreamy; the moustaches full; the beard thick; the nose fine and slightly arched' (my translation). In Graindor's opinion, it is a man already tired and has an air of disillusioned sadness. You may form your own opinion from the illustration (on page 30).

Herodes had reasons to be sad. Only two children survived the early death of his wife, and Elpinice by only a few years. His son was a disappointment to him and the two girls he had developed and affection for were tragically killed. His relations with the Athenians were not always harmonious during his lifetime.

It was, however, another matter after his death, which is thought to have occurred in 177 AD. According to Graindor, 'The Athenians carried his body into the town. The funeral oration by one of Herodes' disciples moved the Athenians to tears. Never had Athens lost such a citizen of such sumptuous generosity. It was never to know such another and, in a sense, it was a funeral oration for Athens itself which was also to die following the disappearance of the man that had succeeded in reviving her during a half century by the force of his talent and fortune.'

Here, beside the Cenotaph he built for the wife who was his partner in many of these achievements, perhaps he found peace during his years as a widower, and could reflect with satisfaction that he had created a fitting tribute to her—perfect in its proportions, beautiful in all its parts; modest yet highly individual. He could not dedicate it to a goddess, for Annia, although likened to one, was not; but he had created a building dedicated to something beyond the human, which may be conceived as being eternal; a love of the beautiful. It is a love which he must have shared with Annia and it has communicated across the centuries.

Every work of the past, be it a poem, painting or, in this case, a building, can be thought of as having a secret rendezvous with the present. It has a time when it emerges from obscurity and becomes understood—what philosopher Walter Benjamin has called a 'now of know-ability'. For Annia Regilla's Cenotaph I believe that time has arrived.

29 *An eighteenth-century engraving*

XX

RETURN FROM ROME. MARRIAGE IN SWEDEN.

The Rome Scholars did not stay in the school during the summer months of July to September and it was soon time to depart. I cannot recall that I did so with sadness. It had been a wonderful experience but I was looking forward to marriage in the autumn, setting up a home in Harlow, and re-joining the community of architects at the Development Corporation to get on with the job of designing a new town. I was also looking forward to the return journey. This time I would not be alone and the days were long and sunny.

First we visited Spoleto Cathedral to see the frescoes by Fra Filippo Lippi (1406-69). In particular we were interested to see an Annunciation, for we, like Fra Filippo himself, had fallen for the young nun who modelled for him. As an unruly orphan he had been brought up in a Catholic monastery and, being found gifted, had become a pupil of Masaccio. When he eloped with his model, Lucrezia, and a son was eventually born to them, only the friendship and powerful patronage of the Medici family saved him, and the pope's dispensation was obtained for them to marry. Lucrezia was his inspiration for several lyrically lovely Madonnas. The most beautiful of them is in the Uffizi.

Then on to the great churches of Assisi for the Giotto frescoes, and to spend some time in the refreshing beauty of the early renaissance art of Florence—quite different from that of Rome. But our funds were running out and Britt's resourceful father telegraphed money from Sweden to a shipping office in Genoa which was our next port of call.

In our hotel there we found ourselves sharing our dining table with a Swedish sea captain. Naturally we told him of our adventures, but were very surprised when we came to reception the next morning to find that he had already paid our bill for dinner and our accommodation!

The remainder of the journey went smoothly—cruising at 45 miles per hour, 45 miles to the gallon—and we parted in Paris: Britt to continue north to Sweden by train to make wedding preparations and I to return to Harlow and move from my fourth-floor bedsitter in the Stow shopping centre to a three-bedroom terrace house in Felmongers.

30 John Graham's painting of the interior and a drawing of the exterior from the west, of Maglarp's beautiful old church.

My return was reported in the *Harlow Citizen* under the heading 'Architect toured Italy in 1931 car' and was an accurate resumé, including the additional information, which I must have volunteered, that 'I only spent £1 on maintenance during that time.' It must have been for expenditure on corks!

A little later, however, turning into a garage forecourt for petrol the steering wheel became loose in my hands. I can feel it now. It was found that the ball at the end of the steering rod had become so worn that it had popped out of its slot. A simple welding repair was all that was needed but I thought of the countless hairpin bends we had safely negotiated with precipitous drops beside us, and I was profoundly grateful.

My parents came with me to Sweden for the wedding. It was the first time they had been abroad, and we went by train as was usual in the early 50s, before the days of mass air travel. Britt was part of a large family who were all assembling for the wedding and, as an only child, I found it not a little confusing at first, especially as her sister and two brothers were a generation older than Britt and now had teenage children.

Language, however, was no problem for Britt's sister and her husband had lived for some time in Newcastle and their English was fluent. Most Swedes then, as now, know English but, being perfectionists by inclination, tend not to use what they know lest they should make mistakes. More importantly, we were included as part of this sizeable family from the outset and, for that, Britt's parents, Alma and Johan, must have been responsible.

We wanted to be married in the small, nearby church, dating from the late 1100s which I had seen on my first visit two years previously. It was, like Annia's cenotaph, built of brick but these were huge in comparison with Roman or even English bricks, and then they were painted with the lime-wash produced from furnace-baked local chalk. This was often renewed so that the churches shone out white against the surrounding fields of grain and the frequently clear blue skies above.

There was only one problem. Maglarp's beautiful old church was rarely used since a new one had been built in the 1900s, but Britt's father, by offering to pay for the small organ to be put in order if the work was done in time for our wedding, changed that. So it was that in September 1954 we walked down a flower-bedecked, packed church to the sound of a Bach pastoral and then heard Britt's opera singer brother, Nils, sing Grieg's *First Meeting* from the small balcony behind us. The Protestant service was short and simple, and did not involve a best man. Two of Britt's young nieces were bridesmaids. Britt had designed her own white bridal dress and, in the delightful Scandinavian tradition, an elegant coronet held her veil in place.

31 John Graham's paintings of two nearby 'white' Skane churches Skegrie Church above, and Stora Hammar's church below.

The dinner that followed for some sixty or so family and guests was held at the farm. Built at the turn of the century, its ground floor rooms were large and high-ceilinged, planned en suite with wide doors and ideal for such entertaining. My speech, I thought, was mostly in Swedish but was subsequently told that it was largely in German—more familiar to me after three years in the army of occupation. Nevertheless, it was heartfelt and this always communicates itself. The small photograph on the dinner menu card was of us both taking tea on the steps of the British School at Rome.

Since we had travelled so much during the past three years we had no wish to go to an exotic place for our honeymoon and spent the week in the tiny seaside town of Torekov where Britt had spent her first happy summer after the time in hospital, companioned by Märta, a singer-actress friend of brother Nils. The small Hotel Kattegat was perfect for us and, with our future home in mind, we found some original Swedish-designed light fittings in the nearby town of Angelholm which still hang in the Harlow house. For the honeymoon Britt's father let us use his American saloon. It had left-hand drive although Sweden, at that time, still drove on the left, so I found myself sitting and driving on the left and changing gear with my right hand—a new combination which, for all my varied driving experiences, I had not previously encountered. It took a little while to reprogramme my thinking.

We returned to England by train, complete with several packages of wedding presents, and hired a London taxi to take us from the station to Harlow. In those days, before England had motorways, the route to Harlow passed through the wilds of Epping Forest. Our London taxi driver, who had probably never heard of Harlow, was no doubt getting increasingly uneasy as dusk came and the twisted hornbeams of the forest began to look, to me at least, increasingly troll-like. He nevertheless, carried on as I assured him that Harlow was just on the other side.

And so, as on other memorable occasions, we completed our journey in the dark. It was not exactly Athens, but I hoped that Britt would settle and it could become our home.

32   Our 50s living room in Felmongers professionally photographed for a promotional brochure

XXI

LIFE IN THE NEW TOWN

Would Britt like living in a new country? I had observed among my architect colleagues that if their wives settled down they stayed in Harlow. If they disliked the experience of living in what could not yet be described as a town, as it was continually under construction, they moved on. Britt had not come from a big city but a 'stand-alone' farm, and had attended school in the harbour town of Trelleborg, mostly built in the nineteenth century and still developing. Pretty villages were not part of her experience, although the sparkling Baltic and sandy beaches close by clearly were.

A partially heated house with troublesome and dirty coal fires took some getting used to. Daily milk deliveries on the doorstep were a compensation. We had the first of Harlow's neighbourhood shopping centres nearby and this provided a butcher, baker, fishmonger and greengrocer, while a post office, branch bank, branch library, two newsagents and a W H Smith catered for other needs. There was a church, a dance hall and an old rectory that had been turned into a community centre. As a sign of things to come this had its forecourt graced by a piece of sculpture, *Chiron*, commissioned by the Development Corporation to commemorate the Coronation of Queen Elizabeth II the previous year.

At that time in Sweden, girls often attended special domestic science courses, but Britt, due to her time in hospital had not done so. She knew, however, how food ought to taste and, armed with an excellent, no nonsense Swedish cookbook, set about learning and noting her successes in it.

The correct ingredients, however, were not always obtainable. I found myself asking for crayfish and being told by the Stow fishmonger that he remembered catching them as a boy, but now they were only obtainable in London. And it was to London we had to go for several of the items to furnish our home.

During those years fogs were frequent and we would drive slowly back through Epping Forest; Britt, having removed the celluloid side window, peering out to follow the kerb-line marking the edge of the road, while I tried to glimpse the 'cats eyes' at intervals marking its centre. Our efforts were rewarded because our living room was found worthy to be professionally photographed for a promotion brochure in the 1950s. Captioned 'a typical interior' it featured the Swedish light fittings, ceramics and textiles we had brought with us. The furniture was mostly Danish and the interior design talent was Britt's as much as mine.

Other aspects of Swedish life which Britt might have missed in her new country were brilliantly overcome by importing part of it for months at a time in the shape of teenage 'au pair' girls. The first of these came about quite naturally when her parents, who were already friends of the family, inquired if their Ingrid could be of help to us. It was a time when Swedish teenagers were keen to come to England. (Nowadays America and places further afield, or well paid vacation jobs are more attractive.) Ingrid, now a grandmother, was the first in a succession of girls over four decades with many of whom we have remained in contact and they have become part of the family, because that is how they were treated. We did not have children, therefore baby-sitting was not required. The girls went everywhere with us, and that included sightseeing, shopping and theatre visits to London which, in those days, was much easier to negotiate by car. Moreover, the front bench seat in the little coupé could accommodate three. Seat belts had not yet been introduced. When Britt's accompanist friend, Elsa, came for a holiday we drove to Wales with her and toured its beauties.

Eventually of course, we needed to change our faithful and flexible vehicle to something more modern and with my parent's financial help bought a 'safari yellow' Hillman convertible which, according to the handbook, had previously been owned by Lady Norwich. Remembering the distances which the little Morris 8 had covered, from the north of Stockholm to Sicily, it was not without a pang of regret mixed with gratitude that I sold it, by then aged twenty-five years, for £25.

With our teenage 'daughters' we had memorable theatre visits and secured autographs from 'stars' such as Maurice Chevalier, Yves Montand and Ginger Rogers, visited Carnaby Street and the Kings Road to sample 'Swinging London' and check whether the mini-skirts were as brief as they were reported to be. They were.

Britt's parents also came each year to spend two or three weeks with us and then we drove back to Sweden and spent our summer holiday on the farm beside the Baltic. I began to get fluent in Swedish.

When Alma and Johan came to England it was by boat from Trelleborg to Tilbury where we met them. Britt's mother would be carrying a large bag full of Swedish specialities such as homemade pâtés and eel from the nearby Baltic where they had an eel-fishing concession. By such means the 'culture shock' between Sweden and England was minimised. Britt, however, never wished to give up her Swedish nationality, nor did I want her to do so. On the contrary, I cherished all links to Sweden.

It is likely that Annia Regilla as a young wife felt the difference less than Britt. She moved from a rich aristocratic family in Rome to a similar household in Athens accompanied by servants and possibly friends. Britt moved from a country where class distinctions had practically disappeared to one where they certainly existed, and still do, providing endless fascination to Scandinavians and others. I had been excellently educated at two grammar schools, one on each side of Manchester, and in these grammar schools class had not been a factor. In the newly forming town of Harlow it was not a factor either, although when I became an employer I found the distinction between employer and employee, notably absent in Sweden, awkward and regrettable, and tried to eliminate it.

The Swedish rules of hospitality, however, were something of a challenge. Britt was naturally hospitable, but when return invitations were not always forthcoming she felt she should not continue. I pointed out that the English take such things more lightly and reciprocate in other ways. In these ways we adjusted to our interracial marriage and there was never a cause for friction. Indeed it was an enrichment to our lives and we grew closer, if that were possible.

There was no lack of culture and entertainment in those early years of the new town. The relatively large proportion of young professionals in the small population ensured that much of it was self-generated. There were madrigal groups and small choirs. I played treble recorder in amateur concerts. A series of special events and talks were arranged by and for the Development Corporation staff and their wives. Frederick Gibberd spoke about his design for Heathrow Airport, which was being done in his London office. Architect Peter Smithson came to speak about his school buildings at Hunstanton in a style labelled 'New Brutalism' then making the headlines. It was not a design approach we were practising in Harlow. The fact that Peter and his wife Alison had purposefully left England in 1951 to get away from what they called 'the horrors' of the Festival of Britain speaks for itself.

The most memorable outing of all was when Britt and I were part of a small group that visited Henry Moore at Much Hadham where he and his wife Irina had come to live some ten years previously. He talked to us in the small garden studio or shed and then left us for a time—surrounded by shelves of pocketable items such as models for sculpture, interestingly shaped stones and bones—while he went to read a bedtime story to his daughter.

In February 1955 the Development Corporation made a submission to the Arts Council for an Art Centre for Harlow and, probably due to my exhibition experience, I was asked to produce a design, including studios for artists and a small gallery building for exhibitions or concerts. Extracts from the draft submission show the aspirations the Corporation had from the outset to develop the arts.

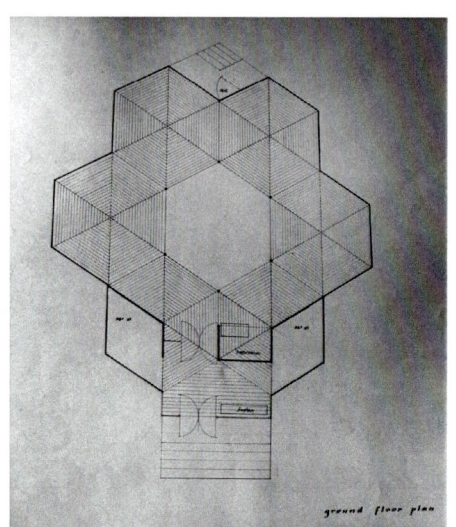

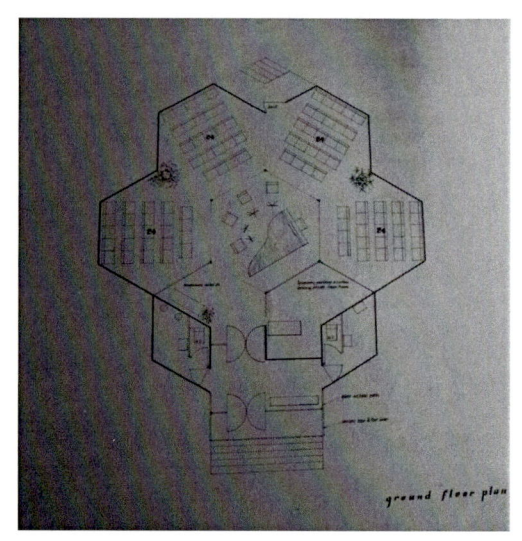

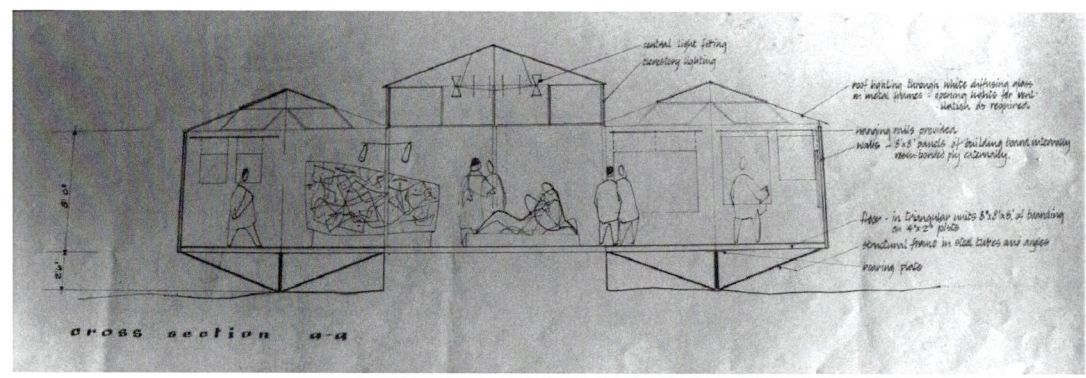

33   *Design drawings by John Graham for the small gallery in the Arts Centre. Proposals submitted by the Development Corporation to the Arts Council in 1955.*

Harlow New town has reached a population of 20,000 and is growing at a rate of 6,000 per year … this very rapidity with which the town is growing and the strictly economic considerations which have governed that development have necessarily left a large debit on the cultural side and one which it is necessary to correct as soon as possible … It is unlikely that the proper civic buildings, including a theatre and concert hall, which form part of the Master Plan, will be built for several years. Meanwhile, this small centre would meet a present need and foster the demand for more elaborate provision in the future. And even when the larger buildings are complete there can be no doubt that a successful Arts Centre with a small hall would continue to serve a useful valuable purpose … . There is already in existence a Harlow Arts Trust, an independent body formed on the initiative of the Corporation and local people, to foster the arts in Harlow. Its aims have hitherto been modest and it has existed primarily to buy pieces of sculpture for the town; for example, a 'Family Group' by Henry Moore has been commissioned and should be ready by the spring. The Trust would however, represent a suitable instrument for receiving the Arts Council's help and for providing a Committee of Management for the Arts Centre.

From neither State nor local Authority can grants be obtained for the development of an Arts Centre. Hence for the fulfilment of this ideal, Harlow must look further afield. It must look at those who believe there is a vital relationship between life and the arts and who can see that in a new town (itself a symbol and expression of the visual arts) this relationship can best be expressed in a building worthy of the cause it serves.

(February 1955)

When Nicolas Pevsner came to talk about his admired series of County Architectural guides some colleagues showed him the design for the Arts Centre. Pevsner glanced at the drawings and commented that he did not care for a 'proliferation of pentagons' a rather glib phrase, I thought (they were actually hexagons). It was several years later, on visiting Henry Playfair's fine neo-classical building in Edinburgh housing Scotland's collection of fine arts that I saw how admirably a 'proliferation of hexagons' worked as exhibition spaces.

Alas, no grant was forthcoming and I took the drawings and draft submission with me when I left the Development Corporation, which I was soon to do. The years 1952-56, including leave of absence for the Rome Scholarship, had been fascinating, and I had moved at my request through all three sections of the Architect's Department, beginning in the Industrial one where I had designed one of the humblest of the new town units—a small group of shops and cafe—and detailed an entrance foyer to a major laboratory building where the prominent staircase was a direct tribute to

34a   Adams House as originally designed by John Graham before the shops were allowed to extend and enclose the colonnade.

b   The design for the tile mural at the south east entrance as carried out but now partly destroyed.

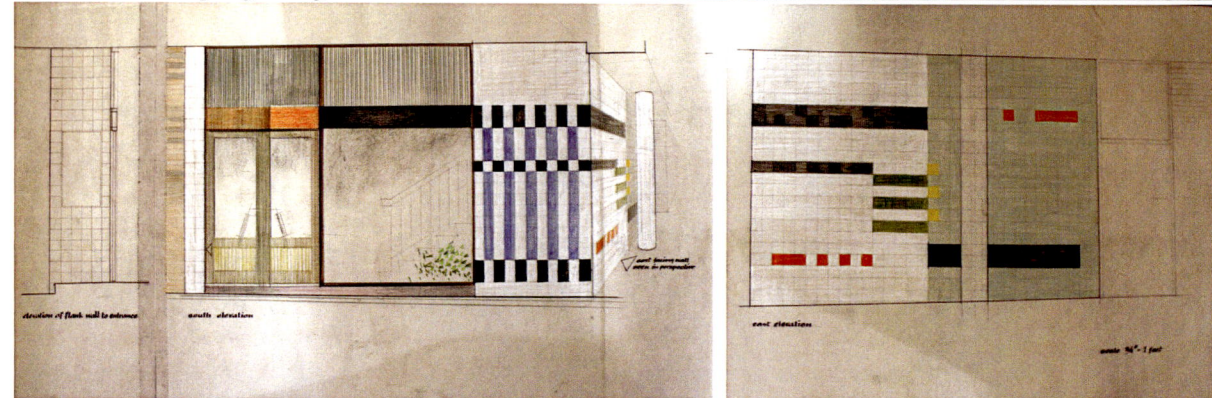

c   The author's drawing of the roof café at first floor level as built and connecting with the Rows but not obscuring the shops.

my most admired Swedish architect, Gunnar Asplund. Next, in the Housing section, together with a colleague from Leeds, we developed one of the first Radburn layouts in the country. Taking its name from the forerunner in America, the principle was to have vehicular access and garages on the garden side so that the homes could face onto greenways and footpaths. When eventually it was built it was named Radburn Close and if more widely used might have reduced the on-street parking problem which resulted from the multiple car-ownership never envisaged when Harlow was planned.

Finally, I moved to the Town Centre section and joined the group working on the Market Square which Gibbered referred to as the 'Principle space or focus for the north of the town centre because of my love of the oldest form of English shopping.' My responsibility was Adams House which formed the eastern side of the square with its colonnade sheltering the approach to the town's main post office, and included a memorial clock on a striped blue and white tiled background. I also designed a tile mural, now partly removed, at the south east entrance. When first completed the square was a lively place with trees, sculpture, seating, removable stalls, and additional shopping at an upper level on the west side, inspired and named after the Chester Rows, and this led onto a first floor open roof café overlooking the space. When the Queen first visited Harlow in the 1950s it was the only part of the Town Centre to be complete.

During my time at the Corporation I had got to know Harlow's Architect Planner when he made his round of the drawing boards on the two or three days a week when he came from Hampstead Garden Suburb where he was living. We found we understood each other on architectural matters and one day in l956, as we walked together across the car park he explained that he was soon to open a branch of his London practice in Harlow and would like me to come and work in it. As I had originally come to Harlow to work with him, my answer was clear, and so my life, and Britt's, was soon to see some changes.

XXII

KEY BUILDINGS IN HARLOW AND NEW HORIZONS

The Harlow office was established so that Frederick Gibberd, or 'FG' as we always called him, could have closer control over the design of key buildings in the new town. At the same time he bought a property on its northern fringe which would be his house, garden and drawing studio. For the new office to be on a sound financial footing, contracts outside Harlow were also allocated to it. During the next twenty-seven years that the offices existed my horizons would, therefore change, although Harlow remained the focus.

It was the same for Britt and even for her parents when they were staying with us, because they would accompany me on site visits. We became very familiar with the route to Huddersfield where the various stages of the post-war expansion of its College of Technology stretched over a ten year period. The stone which gives this northern town so much of its character was used in all the college buildings and the Music School which was one of the last stages was for me the most interesting. Working closely with an acoustic consultant we detailed soundproof practice rooms and a small, octagonal, concert hall for rehearsals of full orchestra and choir, or concerts by soloists and chamber music groups.

In the move from the Development Corporation and involvement in running contracts I naturally lost some of the design freedom I had enjoyed but, as the years went by, could increasingly make a contribution.

During the same period we would also pay visits to Bath where the Technical College (www.c20society.org.uk/bolm/bath-technical-college) was being built in the historic centre, close to the Abbey and the Royal Baths. Here, again, stone facing was used throughout the design but this was the creamy Bath stone used to cover the structural frame unlike Huddersfield. When the third and final stage came, FG was at full stretch and entrusted it to me and I could design the Assembly Hall as a hexagonal building and venue for small orchestras and chamber music groups.

We had begun to think of building our own house, primarily because we wanted to live on one level with easy access to the garden. I have always thought that stairs in a dwelling have only disadvantages and are better done without! But I knew that an individually designed, one-off, house would be costly because it lacked the element of repetition. The answer came when we went to buy a fortepiano to accompany Britt's singing. A colleague, clarinettist, told us of W H Colt, director of the firm that made prefabricated cedar houses, who during the war years, when production paused, used to buy such pianos and restore them to rescue them from conversion into dressing tables. I already knew of Colt Houses as traditional designs, admirably suited to village and rural sites, but when we arrived at their showplace in Bethersden, Kent, and duly bought a handsome instrument, I was surprised to find a completely new Colt house type—a single storey 'Festival Bungalow' which had been inspired, as so much else, by the 1951 celebration and designed for the company by architect Osborne in a refreshingly contemporary style with generous room sizes and wide windows with cills practically at ground level. The modular design and range of alternative finishes, inside and out, offered great flexibility and the costs of the kit were comparatively modest. This was the solution.

Sweden, with its dry climate and many forests, is a land of timber buildings and it seemed a natural type of house to us, and south east England is one of its driest areas, although as we found not to be compared to Sweden in this respect.

Then we went looking for a suitable site and found—a tree! A mighty oak, at least five hundred years in age, and probably many more, it stood in a hedge and brook boundary on the northern edge of Latton Common, in one of the sites allocated for private development at the end of a small cul-de-sac of Development Corporation designed detached houses. Once we were on the site and looked at the great multi-branched tree and the view of the common gently rising to woodland on its horizon we knew where our living room windows would be placed.

The site was purchased freehold and the cost, even with my many modifications and additions, could be met with the help of a bank loan, for mortgages, like staircases in my opinion, are to be avoided if at all possible. The timber parts arrived in two lorries on Bonfire Night to the cul-de-sac, and I was relieved when they were safely unloaded the next day, and spread around the site ready for the sympathetic builder, who had already prepared the foundations, to begin assembling a huge jigsaw puzzle. It only took a few months and we moved in during the spring of 1960.

Britt kept up her daily singing practice with pianist and singer friends, but the opportunities which had been available to her in Sweden, where it was normal for meetings, fashion shows and re-union dinners, even political talks, to be graced by a singer, did not exist. We gave at-home concerts for our friends and Britt enlarged her repertoire, which already included many songs by Grieg and other Scandinavian composers, by the delightful Bergerettes, written for Marie Antoinette and her friends as they played at being shepherds and shepherdesses in the gardens of Versailles. She also discovered Erik Satie's beautiful songs and the cabaret songs of Charles Trenet.

Meanwhile, I had been asked by the Christian Science community in the area to find a suitable site in Harlow and design a church for services and meetings. Neighbourhood sub-centres are provided throughout the Master Plan—small groups of shops with places for a pub and a community building. In one of these a site was found, opposite a school and beside a wide green area which swept up to a handsome fifteenth-century church. Here Henry Moore's *Harlow Family Group* first stood before it was moved into the town centre. My design inside and out, used a special sandlime brick which I had discovered, and was topped with a roof of Roman pantiles. It was reminiscent of small churches in Denmark and southern Sweden, although who would know? The acoustics were excellent, and Britt was the regular soloist—the solo being a normal part of the service, before the two readers read a lesson-sermon fresh each week from the Mother Church in Boston. For many years I served as one or the other of the two readers and it was an inspiring time for us both. Reflecting on it now, I can see a parallel in some respects to the Annia/Herodes partnership in Athens stadium.

We discovered the delights of London's most intimate recital room, the Wigmore Hall, and besides the piano, lieder and chamber music concerts heard master classes for singers given by Tito Gobbi, Elisabeth Schwarzkopf, Brigitta Fassbender and others. When the National Theatre opened we were thrilled by the masterpiece of architecture that it is and the rich variety of plays, including the ancient classics, given in its Greek-inspired Olivier Theatre. After she came to live in London we could follow one of our favourite actresses, Ingrid Berman, in her frequent stage appearances, and watch Ginger Rogers tirelessly signing autographs at Drury Lane Theatre stage door after her performance in *Mame*. A sequence of musicals was to be enjoyed, from Sondheim's *Company* onwards, and perhaps the eight times we saw *Guys and Dolls* with different casts over the years at the National Theatre were the high points—or were the jazz concerts at the Festival Hall by Stan Getz or the Oscar Petersen Trio? I felt we were experiencing some sort of Golden Age and recorded these nights in a series of small notebooks.

The town was taking shape, and in the office I was contributing to Harlow's key buildings. The first purpose-designed community sportcentre to be built in England was designed with the utmost economy and simplicity. Cost comparisons with others built in the 1960s and later showed Harlow's costs to be less than half of any other. My suggestion to use the special light grey sandlime brick which I had used for the church, and parts of our own house, was adopted. The main space was found to have excellent acoustics for large choral concerts and housed them for over forty years

35   *The church at Ward Hatch designed by John Graham for the Christian Science community*

until its demolition. On the nearby Willow Beauty public house I had a free hand and gave it a roof terrace overlooking the cricket pitch.

Harlow's first town hall was to have been fourteen stories high with a circular council chamber projecting towards the open landscape, but accommodation approved by the council was more modest; the tower height was reduced and the circular council chamber indefinitely postponed. The building was, however, given extra height and identity by being topped by an outlook pavilion housing an exhibition explaining the town below. This I detailed with a barrel-vaulted roof and sheathed the concrete with white Italian glass mosaic—ideas which I had brought back with me from Rome.

The original village of Old Harlow had to be redeveloped if its shopping was to survive competition from the new building in the town. Once the original proposals by FG had been approved by the Development Corporation in 1963 the job was given to the Harlow Office. I remained in charge throughout a series of contracts involving many restorations and a few new buildings, but never demolition. Patience was the quality most needed, for it was a step by step process proceeding without any coercion of traders over a twelve-year period, until finally the traffic could be removed and the paving pattern, which I designed, of alternating red brick and concrete slabs stretched across the precinct between the shop fronts. The end result, however, was widely acclaimed, being given a Civic Trust Award in 1971 and in 1975 one of the only twenty European Architecture Heritage Awards.

In the market area of Old Harlow the conversion of the late nineteenth-century maltings and nearby schoolhouse into a campus for the University of Newfoundland was wholly given to me to design. It would be good, FG said, for me to get him 'out of my hair' for a time, and on completion this received a Civic Trust commendation.

In 1965, following the departure of Gerard Goalen into private practice, David Roberto and I were invited to become partners. And now we met monthly at the London Office in Percy Street to review all our contracts and afterwards adjourn to a nearby French restaurant. On the way back to Harlow I was often to drive FG, and on these journeys we did not talk about architecture but another subject of mutual interest. He was very pleased to have become a member of the Royal Academy and could exhibit work from the partnership at the annual Summer Show. He was adding to his collection of watercolours and drawings by living British artists. Many of these were bought from Academy exhibitions and eventually donated to the town and exhibited in a gallery space which we created at first floor level in the original town hall. Britt and I also visited the London galleries and the RA Summer Exhibitions to buy paintings, prints and sculpture for our new home and in this way made friendships with artists Peter Wickham and James Butler RA.

36   An early photograph of Harlow's original town hall

37 The Community Sports Centre interior

38 The redeveloped Harlow Village High Street on completion

39   Harvey Centre main mall

40   Longman Publishers headquarters building

The award-winning publicity given to the redevelopment of Old Harlow had led to the practice being chosen to design a new shopping centre for Banbury where the conservation and integration of the existing Market Square was an important factor. FG's initial planning, as always, established the strong pedestrian routes interconnecting existing shopping, parking and bus station which would ensure the new development's commercial success. Conflict between shoppers and goods deliveries was avoided by taking vehicles up a ramp onto the roof of the shops where their upper floors received deliveries. The large areas of blank external walling, however, presented a problem. I proposed to resolve it by restoring Banbury Castle to the town. The castle had stood on this exact site but had been razed by the town's citizens following the Civil War. This is not the sort of idea which FG would have initiated, but it was approved at a monthly partners' meeting, and Banbury eventually received a reminder of its former castle, in brick rather than stone. The Duke of Gloucester at the opening in 1977 showed his architectural education by quizzing me about the 'machicolation' and my drawings were shown in an RA Summer Exhibition.

The servicing of shops at the first floor level was to prove relevant when the Harlow office was designing the commercial development in the southern part of the Town Centre. Since the original Master Plan the town had become a Regional Centre, car ownership greatly increased and supermarkets were demanding more space. The essentials; the Market Square linked by Broad Walk to the Civic Centre and Water Gardens, were to remain but the shopping became more dense taking the form of an enclosed two-level mall incorporating a multi-storey car park.

FG thought, we all thought, that this would be the completion of the Town Centre apart from the arts and entertainment building in the Civic Square for which funding had not yet been found. Future expansion, FG believed, would take place vertically enhancing the urban character and making the Town Centre a finer visual focus for the town.

The Harvey Centre, named after the town's general manager from 1955-73, was the largest single contract ever let by the Corporation and proved to be the most difficult and dramatic. It would occupy the Harlow Office of the partnership for six years. It would also be its swansong, and I would find myself standing trial defending the design at a public inquiry.

41   Harvey Centre main mall at Christmastime. Antanas Brzdys's 8 metre high polished stainless steel sculpture standing in its fountain pool—the town's meeting place.

XXIII

THE HARVEY CENTRE COMPLETES THE PLAN

Totally enclosed air-conditioned shopping centres had been built in America and this was the type adopted for Harlow. The first scheme which was approved in 1974, had shopping raised on a deck approached by escalators, with servicing at ground level; but rising inflation and falling rent expectations indicated that this would prove too expensive. A redesign was done with the shops at ground level and the servicing from the first floor roof, as at Banbury. This was a much better design, but gave rise to violent objections as it involved the closure of Cross Street and presented a problem with servicing the Playhouse. This problem the Corporation planners proposed to solve with a new service road around St Paul's church, which raised new objections. The Playhouse Supporters' Club distributed a sensational leaflet at each performance:

> At enormous expense! By public demand? Coming shortly? THE DEAD CENTRE OF HARLOW. Produced by the Harlow Development Corporation. From designs by Sir Frederick Gibberd.

They collected many signatures and to the Corporation's dismay the Department of the Environment decided that a public inquiry should be held into the road closure.

The inquiry took place in August 1977, and the barrister retained by the Church authorities effectively presented all the objectors' arguments over a period of four days. The presiding inspector, seeing that there was an unresolved problem with the road framework decided against the scheme, but the Department of the Environment deferred its decision and allowed the inquiry to be re-opened to consider alternative proposals. They were now prepared. The service road by the church disappeared and an extension to the Playhouse including a large lift for deliveries of scenery to the Playhouse workshops was introduced. This was now to be explained to the opposition and agreements sought before the inquiry re-opened on 14 May 1978.

I had separate meetings with the Playhouse Trust and the Playhouse Supporters' Club to remove their fears about the practicability of the lift; and also with the church authorities at their office in Westminster.

I was well prepared, metaphysically, for these meetings and Britt's support was crucial. Our expectation of harmony was borne out and without exception all parties were prepared to accept the new scheme. When the inquiry re-opened only private objectors and the local rector, Canon Knight, remained to be convinced.

I was chosen as the only architectural witness to present and then defend the design, as Sir Frederick's connections with the Development Corporation made him suspect. This time, fully aware how vital the matter was, the Corporation engaged a top-flight barrister, a Queen's Counsel, and I visited his chambers in Lincoln's Inn Fields, to prepare a brief for my presentation at the inquiry.

With the recent meetings fresh in mind, I was confident and welcomed the opportunity to explain the scheme and to describe how the central space, which was much larger than required for commercial purposes, was intended to be a town space for meetings and exhibitions and would be furnished with seats and planting and have a water feature and other sculpture. It would remain open after the shops had closed in order to provide the route from the Playhouse to the bus station. The large lift for Playhouse scenery deliveries, which had been accepted as practical, would remove the threat of disturbance to Sunday morning services.

It was nevertheless unpleasant, under the cross questioning from objectors, to be accused of proposing a 'concrete monstrosity'. On the contrary, as I explained, this was largely an infill scheme and the external walls, where they appeared between existing buildings, would be of distinctively shaped precast units, identifying the Harvey Centre, with polished surfaces of crushed natural stone.

During a pause I found myself sitting next to the local rector and asked him why he still opposed the scheme while others had been persuaded to change their minds. He appeared to doubt the truth of their change of heart and when I mentioned that I thought that he was in the conversion business his only reply was 'original sin'. With that our conversation ended. His subsequent cross-questioning by counsel together with the other objectors left no doubt of the successful outcome.

The Corporation's General Manager, Andrew Bardsley, was heard whistling down the corridor the next morning and for a while I was the local hero and was seated next to Henry Moore at a celebratory dinner.

The office, however, still had to detail the revised scheme and during the long delay several existing stores which would be integrated had changed their requirements and the office team had been partially disbanded. We were still making revisions after construction started but the Centre opened for the essential Christmas trading in 1981. If it had not done so I would have been held responsible and the local hero's head would have been on the block!

With its high central space and multi-level shopping it was not unlike the Markets of Trajan in Rome, and young Annia Regilla would have enjoyed shopping there as teenagers do today, although I doubt if the variety of goods on offer could match those in imperial Rome. When it opened there was, indeed, a water feature. FG's first idea had been to contact the sculptor responsible for the moving metal sculpture outside the Sea and Ships Pavilion on the Festival of Britain South Bank and this is what I indicated on an early sketch of the interior, but worries about splashing made him change his mind and contact Antanas Brazdys who designed a great bird of polished stainless steel which was to unfold its wings in the roof space. The maquette of the striking design was immediately approved by the Corporation Board and was to form part of the building contract. I designed the fountain pool in which it was to stand and surrounded it with a circular wall at sitting height so that it could become a meeting place, as it did for many years, complete with 'three coins in the fountain' activity which provided income for charity. The sculpture, some 25 feet (8m) high, was probably the largest indoor modern work in the country. As it was part of the building contract, the approval of stage payments to the sculptor was my responsibility and I remember travelling with Britt to Gloucestershire to one of the few steelworks in the country which had presses large enough to put the required curvature on the great wings in order to check that this had been done. The sculpture was so large that we could not complete one of the entrances until it had been installed. I remember thinking that it would not be removed before the building was demolished. I was to be proved wrong.

With the successful opening of the Harvey Centre FG's Master Plan for Harlow was virtually complete, but he had added an element. The international firm Longmans, Green & Co., who had been publishing in London since 1724 had already made the decision to move their headquarters to Harlow and had appointed Sir Frederick as their architect. In view of the high quality building they were prepared to finance and their need for London connections they were offered a site immediately opposite the town station where there had previously been no development. It would be a gateway to Harlow; the first view to those arriving by train and a landmark on the approach along the Stort Valley.

I was now a partner and closely involved with the preparation of the original designs. The client's brief showed an overwhelming need for individual offices and little demand for larger spaces.

There were superb views; northwards over the River Stort to open countryside and southwards to the town park. In the design the projecting bays allowed the mental relief of landscape views to be enjoyed from every office. The large precast storey-height units forming the facades each weighed over four tonnes, and were specified to have a white cement and Portland stone aggregate fine-spun to a smooth finish. The firm which had the required skill and material to produce such units was on the Isle of Portland itself and they got the contract. Britt and I enjoyed our visit to Weymouth to inspect and approve production.

The entrance foyer, clearly visible across from the station, had finishes of the highest quality including flooring of grey-green Broughton Moor slate and Botticino marble wall linings. The spectator could also see through to the central courtyard where the Henry Moore bronze which Longmans owned had been placed. I recall the day when Moore arrived to meet Longman's director Sir John Newsum and myself to place the piece. It took a considerable time, and I realised that Moore was much more comfortable in landscape than architectural surroundings.

FG considered Longman House to be his best building in Harlow. It was the only one to receive a special feature article in *The Architectural Review* and, because of its advanced use of precast concrete units, in an Italian specialist journal. 'Iconic' was not in those days the fashionable term it has since become, but it could have been justly applied to this building. It would also have complied with Plotinus' criteria on 'The Beautiful'.

As Britt and I drove back to Harlow from Hertford along the Stort Valley Longman House was our landmark by day and night for many years. We felt that we were now driving back to a town, a town which we had seen take shape, had used, understood and enjoyed and would not willingly exchange for another.

XXIV

WORKING WITH FREDERICK GIBBERD

'Blessed is the person who has built a new city.' This line, which Herodes Atticus added to his inscription on the Gate of Eternal Harmony after his wife Annia Regilla died, could be applied to Sir Frederick Gibberd. Unlike any other of the post-war new towns he remained its guiding designer throughout. The relationship of the building to landscape, the green wedges or 'lungs' which separate the neighbourhoods and give Harlow the high proportion of open space which only now is being recognised as essential for a 'healthy' town, the 'humane' grouping of mixed developments, houses with gardens, streets forming spaces enlivened by sculpture, a network of community buildings and a town centre focus easily reached on foot or by bicycle, all this, and much more, must have given him satisfaction, despite the setbacks and necessary compromises.

This he could reflect on as he tended the six acres of garden he was creating at the end of Marsh Lane. It was there I would drive, along the unsurfaced, pot-holed, blind cornered lane to check design drawings or receive the latest batch, and I would find him, as likely as not, on his knees in some green spot. I will not say 'weather permitting', for weather rarely stopped his work of creating those 'outdoor rooms' furnished with sculpture or architectural fragments or large pots. When we got inside to the drawing board there was often a new painting to be noted and, in the final years, a growing collection of large Edmund Rubbra watercolours close-hung on the walls of the large room. Parties for the office staff and their wives were given in the summer and on Bonfire Night, but 'no bangers' was the rule.

The range of work handled by the Gibberd practice was truly phenomenal, from an ecumenical chapel to a cathedral and mosque, from power stations to reservoirs, colleges, shopping centres, factories and offices, from an airport to a New Town. Nearly every contract was a fresh challenge. There were usually several in progress in the Harlow office in various stages of design or construction. My twenty-seven years there were a busy time with few moments to remember Rome or the inconclusive story surrounding the building I measured. Britt and I did revisit briefly in

42   Watercolour of Collioure where Derain and Matisse inaugurated Fauvism, by John Graham.

43   In the olive grove of Les Collettes next to Renoir's house, by John Graham.

1972 staying opposite the beautiful early Christian church of Santa Sabina and we went out to the Campagna to check on Annia Regilla's temple/tomb. We found a few minor repairs had been done and some telltales put across small cracks to check any further movement. Otherwise little had changed. The farm was still there, and the family remembered us, although the fig tree against the wall had disappeared and they were amused that I could recall it. Their subsequent postcard sent us greetings from 'noi del tempio'.

In the late seventies, with partners' agreement, I entered an international competition for the design of a Christian Science care home in the little town of Rolle on the southern shore of Lake Geneva. The first prize would have been the commission, and I did the work in the Harlow office assisted by David Ives. We were placed second and I received a substantial sum of Swiss francs which I shared with my fellow partners, somewhat to their surprise. This helped finance a week's visit to Paris in April 1979 so Britt could celebrate her 50th birthday there and in the Louvre we found and contemplated the handsome marble carving of Herodes Atticus from his estate at Marathon. On return I was impelled to borrow the 1930 biography by Graindor from the Society of Antiquaries and attempt my own translation from the French. The story of Annia and Herodes was becoming clearer, although there was precious little about Annia.

FG liked to go on brief study trips with his landscape architect friend Geoffrey Jellicoe and we would approve his expenses at our subsequent partners' meetings. At one of these he proposed that we others should take a 'sabbatical' of, say, three months when we could so arrange our work. This typically enlightened proposal both David Roberts and I took advantage of, but none of the other partners ever did.

Britt and I decided to use our sabbatical time to visit painters' workplaces. We followed Van Gogh south to Provence, stayed in Arles, and visited the Camargue—that unique area of reed-fringed lagoons full of croaking frogs, where white horses waded and groups of small black bulls or sheep are herded by bereted and bronzed mounted shepherds. Here, near the town of Saintes-Marie-de-la-mer, Van Gogh painted the boats drawn up on the great beach. It was his first view of the Mediterranean. From Arles we went to nearly St Rémy, to the Priory hospital where he was confined for a year after his quarrel with Gauguin and self-wounding. It had beautiful cloisters and a walled garden where Van Vogh painted those irises. Beyond were cypresses and the crazily shaped little hills—les Alpilles. Britt was reading his letters from St Remy and commented: 'how sane and sensible he sounds.'

At Aix-en-Provence we could see Cézanne's studio as he left it in 1906, the apples of the still lifes replaced with matching new ones as the old decayed. Nearby were his palette and paint box, satchel, black hat and stick. There was a large north light, with a curtain to draw across, and

44   Britt beside Renoir's bronze of wood nymph 'Pomona'

the walls were coloured grey. In the woods of Tholonet where he loved to paint we found the occasionally leaning pine trees, varied greens, red earth and rocky outcrops all present, and in the distance was the great silhouette of Mt St Victoire.

We stayed for several days in Collioure where Derain and Matisse discovered shadowless Fauvism and I tried to recapture some of their boldness.

In the olive grove of 'les Collettes' which Renoir bought to build a house for his final years we spent hours. I painted the trees standing in pools of shadow among the long grass, sprinkled with flowers and visited by bees, butterflies, and a girl who wheeled out a canopied pram and sat beside it. This was Renoir's outdoor studio. Inside the generously elegant but unostentatious house were well proportioned rooms, marble stairs and fireplaces, beige or light green coloured walls. In the studio, beside his special wheelchair and easel, a couch for the model, not unlike a four-poster bed. Outside on the terrace, with a superb view below of the Baie des Anges and the Cap d'Antibes, was a bronze of the wood nymph Pomona and even a fallen orange to be picked up and placed in her hand.

There were many such illuminating experiences, but perhaps the most moving was in Auvers-sur-Oise where, after visiting the house, now a restaurant, where, in a small upstairs room Van Gogh slowly died after shooting himself, we went up to the small walled cemetery among the fields of ripening corn where Theo and Vincent's simple headstones stand, side by side, of identical shape and almost identical inscription united by a thick bed of evergreen ivy which grows over them both.

This trip, though we knew it not, was to be an inspiration for the fundamental change which was to come about in our lives and the lives of many others working in Harlow. Expansion plans to take the town beyond its population of 80,000 had been in preparation for several years by FG, working with the Development Corporation and the Council, and by 1973 it had seemed that the government approval was finally in sight, but in a short time, governments came and went, and those making the decisions changed with bewildering rapidity as recorded in *Harlow, the Story of a New Town*, published in 1980. Interest had shifted to inner cities. New towns were out of favour; they were to be restrained. A more modest expansion proposal was submitted to the public inquiry, in the summer of 1976 and the Corporation was represented by Queen's Counsel with FG and others giving evidence. It lasted four weeks and the Corporation, confident of a successful outcome, began preliminary work, but had to wait until April 1977 for a decision, and then, it proved negative! There was to be no planned expansion and within a year the Harlow Development Corporation was informed that the date for termination of all its activities was 1980. The Corporation found the decision inconceivable and devastating. Expert teams were suddenly dispersed. Over thirty years later it can clearly be seen how gravely mistaken the decision was. There was already a housing shortage, which has continued to grow: house prices, which had been stable for a decade or more, began to rise in the 1980s and have continued to rise steadily ever since until now the cost of housing is a social problem. The government expected developers to meet the shortfall but this they could not do or did not want to do despite great relaxations of planning permission which have caused local consternation. The crisis now is of a dimension similar to that when the New Towns first started.

The dissolution of the Corporation would also contribute to the closure of the Harlow office, for the London partners could see that there would be no significant work from that source. We had been fully extended on completing the Harvey Centre and there were no other major jobs in progress, nor, because of sharing jobs with the London office, had we become established as a regional practice. The three London partners decided to close the office in 1983. FG was not part of this decision as he was no longer a partner, having retired to become a consultant in 1978. It was expected that I would go to work in London with the other partners, continuing to live in Harlow or get a flat in London. Jobs were offered to the staff but very few took them up. Now in my late 50s and having spent thirty years of an architectural career based in Harlow I was not prepared to start commuting, which was not part of the New Town concept as I saw it and besides, I had an alternative in mind. I decided to resign from the partnership and, after a farewell dinner at the Ritz, where I was presented with a rare and beautiful book—a biography of my Swedish architect hero Gunner Asplund—I saw little of Sir Frederick. During his illness at the house during which, he let it be known that he didn't wish to be visited, he did make exception for one of his first partners, Bob Double, who had been the essential and sympathetic link between the London and Harlow offices. They talked, Bob told me later, only about a current job for which FG was writing a report. Work was his life.

It was shortly afterwards, in April 1983, that I was invited to give a talk at Harlow Museum about Sir Frederick. In the audience was his widow Lady Pat Gibberd who could, as I said, speak about a very different partnership than the working relationship I was to speak of. I was therefore pleased and moved to get a card saying, 'You pitched it just right—it was all very good and delightful. I really enjoyed it … '

It was not a funeral oration, therefore, but as I look back now I am reminded of the words spoken of Herodes Atticus:

'Never had Athens lost such a citizen of such sumptuous generosity. It was never to know such another, and in a sense, it was funeral oration for Athens itself.' Rhetoric is no longer fashionable but the parallels apply. Sir Frederick was generous to a sumptuous degree in the way he devoted his talents to Harlow over a period of over three decades and with his departure the town entered a period where some of its best features would disappear or be threatened.

45   The headstones of the Van Gogh brothers—Vincent and Theo—in the hillside cemetery above Auvers-sur-Oise beneath a cover of evergreen ivy.

46   Ibiza in 1949 was 'an unspoilt island of white cubist houses under African light' and I first began painting daily, as recorded in my unpublished journal 'Franco's Spain'.

XXV

A NEW CAREER

The seeds of the new career I had in mind when the Harlow office of the Frederick Gibberd partnership was closed in 1983 had been growing for many years.

While a student at Manchester University School, together with Dick Felton, I had organised annual exhibitions in the school's life drawing studio of architectural photographs taken by students during our summer vacations. Provincial Exhibitions Ltd had also commissioned me to design the 'modern' dream house in their annual Ideal Homes Exhibitions. I forget how this came about, but it continued for several years. Then, in our graduation year, three of us were asked to design an exhibition where selected items from Manchester Museum would be displayed under the title: 'Primitive Art' in the Whitworth Art Gallery.

We decided to create special spaces by lowering the ceiling and arranging screens with special lighting, colour and plants to suit the very varied character of the exhibits, which included small ivory carvings from the Arctic, Navaho Indian blankets, Australian aborigine boomerangs, Maori carvings and African masks. I designed the invitation card, and together with Peter Liley and Joe Baker made a scale model of our scheme. A quotation from Herbert Read was placed on the red entrance screen. In 1952 the exhibition was unusual for its time and caused much public interest. For me, it was unforgettable.

Naturally, my final thesis was a design for a Regional Exhibition Centre in Manchester's Piccadilly and these exhibition activities, in a unique way, had helped me get to Harlow Development Corporation, for that was the one place I wished to work after getting qualified. I scanned the job advertisements and soon found one, but applicants would need to have prepared working drawings for large-scale housing contracts, something I had not done. One vacancy, however, was for someone with exhibition experience. I applied, was given an interview and got a job. It was the only job application I have ever made.

During my years at the Corporation, as related earlier, I did the design for an arts centre, studios and exhibition building which had been submitted for an Arts Council grant, and while in the Gibberd practice had designed the pavilion exhibition which crowned Harlow's first town hall, and in the evenings had served on the advisory panel for exhibitions within the Playhouse.

Moreover, I had discovered painting independently of architectural presentations. This came about in student days when, in the summer vacation of 1949, together with Tom Markus, I visited Franco's Spain to find out how the third fascist dictator was managing to survive the post-war period. We found a troubled, divided country with the wounds of the Civil War still very much in evidence and I recorded my impressions in a diary/journal. In a two-week visit to Ibiza, in the days before it had any tourist hotels and could only be reached by boat, I had found an unspoilt island of white cubist houses under African light and had begun to paint daily.

All these activities were a preparation for what was to come, and the year of the Rome Scholarship living in a community largely composed of artists was particularly formative, but the defining experience came when Britt and I first visited the Penwith Society in St Ives. In following the development of modern art in England, we were aware of the move, in 1939, out of London to Cornwall, of the Russian-born constructivist Naum Gabo together with Ben Nicholson and Barbara Hepworth and the eventual foundation of the Penwith Society in St Ives to display their abstract art—its beautiful shapes, colour and rhythmical relationships.

After penetrating the maze of tiny streets behind the harbour we found a superbly lit, characterful gallery in a former pilchard warehouse. The paintings and sculpture on display were all and only by Penwith Society members and of consistently high quality. In these surroundings one's vision sharpened. The space was presided over by Kathleen Watkins whose striking appearance and firmness was combined with great warmth and helpfulness. Kathy was the central point of contact for us to meet the artists around and we bought works from John Wells, Paul Mount and Wilhelmina Barns-Graham, a key figure, who had been instrumental in persuading Ben Nicholson and Barbara Hepworth to come to St Ives and found the society, whose first president had been Herbert Read.

So, when the opportunity came to take over the office and open an art gallery in the town centre, I was ready, and it was clear to me that I should use the space, primarily, to bring St Ives to Harlow.

I negotiated retirement terms with my fellow partners which included taking over the remaining years of a fixed rental lease on the office and I received encouraging approval from the Council for a change of use, but objection came from an unexpected source. The Commission for the New Towns, who had taken over the more lucrative assets in the town following the dissolution of the Development Corporation, wrote to say; 'The Commission is principally concerned to preserve the value of its property assets and takes a view that this would be adversely affected by the change of use you request.' The Commission was not interested in cultural or social gains. At that moment I saw clearly that the future of Harlow was no longer in safe or sympathetic hands.

I did not, however, give up and went to see them in London. A compromise was reached by which I would sacrifice the lease after three years, after which it would be let at a higher rental. Now I could write to the chairman of the Penwith Society, Roy Walker, outlining a programme of exhibitions and I got a heart-warming reply: 'How exciting, the news that you intend to open a gallery in Harlow. I do wish you every success with the venture and will be glad to support you in any way that I am able … '

There was no time to be lost. The office was cleared. No partitions needed to be moved for I had designed the original layout and knew that it would work.

I had display panels put over parts of the large windows and exhibition lighting installed. We opened in the spring of 1983 with an appropriately named show: 'Flora' and the following eighteen exhibitions included works by twenty-three St Ives Penwith Society artists, among them Wilhelmina Barns-Graham, John Wells, Roy Walker, June Miles, Jane O'Malley and Paul Mount. My former secretary, Mary Taylor, was invaluable in the day-to-day running of the gallery and previous members of staff helped in other ways and at the private views which were usually held in the evenings. Britt had been involved in my architectural activities as far as possible, but she could now be my partner in all aspects of running a gallery, not only in Harlow, but also during our visits to Cornwall as these extracts from my Gallery Journal show:

> 'What physical characteristic is one most aware of in the case of artists?' Britt queried on our misty drive back from St Ives. I replied, and rightly, that it was the eyes. We had fresh in our mind the strong blue gaze of Wilhelmina Barns-Graham during our afternoon with her; the lively twinkle of Roy Ray when we discussed matters in the car overlooking Porthmeor Beach and the clear eyed Roy Walker during our lunch with him and his wife Peggy.

That was in September 1983. The following April we had arranged to meet Jane O'Malley in her studio:

> The day was brilliantly sunny with a light breeze from the north-east—the sort of weather they have been having for three weeks down here … we looked at work for her solo show at the gallery in November, beginning with the large canvases and proceeding through medium sized oils and gouaches, some drawings and a

pastel, to tiny works for our intimate corner. About seventy works and a sheer delight! What fresh colour relationships, piquantly placed forms, fluency and variety … Jane is our Matisse, and extraordinary to think that she has not yet had a solo show outside Cornwall. Tony O'Malley joined us, gentle and twinkling, but worried, by a possible legal tangle with an unscrupulous sounding dealer in Ireland. He would prefer just to paint his canvases and roll them away rather than be involved in all the rest—showing and selling. Britt sat in the sun by the house steps opposite, talking to Tony, while I went up to John Emanuel's studio to choose work for his input to the 'Nudes' theme show in July. I chose six big torsos. He came with me to Britt and we all sat on the steps as the sun descended; discussed gallery matters and then the St Ives people. Patrick Heron passed and gave a cheery wave … the conversation turned to John Wells with whom John Emanuel had, as he put it, an unobtrusive friendship; John W would contact John E and then they went on picnics … or to air shows where the Red Arrows have inspired drawings—smoke and looping curves. John W was reportedly very fit and in his seventies—not selling except for releasing an occasional work to the Penwith. John E thought he had 'got it right.'

We had a tight schedule: a new show every month with a private view at the beginning, three weeks of viewing, and the last week for hanging the new exhibition. The artists usually came to the opening and had sent me their mailing lists so that visitors came from all over the region. The artists were also responsible for bringing work to the gallery and collecting it. We provided hospitality and, for those who wished to stay—overnight accommodation in a substantial pavilion I had designed in the garden as an alternative to having a country cottage 'retreat'. We had fascinating conversations with our guests and on one occasion Paul Mount accompanied Britt on the piano in two of her Erik Satie waltz songs.

I had intentionally given a plural name: 'John Graham Fine Arts' to the gallery venture. Paul Tompkins came from Enfield to give an audio-visual show with twin projectors and synchronised music. The powerful blend of music and image was effective and beautiful. A Harlow poet, Frederick Vanson, read from his work and the Gallery printed and sold a booklet of *Essex Images* by local artists who had been invited to illustrate his poems and mine. I had also discovered the wonderful world of Swedish lyric poetry and my translations and other poems were on sale.

Frederick Vanson was a long-time friend of the poet and playwright, Christopher Fry, whose verse plays we had seen in London theatres and we were able to book him to come and talk to a full audience on 'Finding a Language'; something he confessed was as yet unpublished when many listeners requested copies. This was one of the high points, but there were many.

All the artists, I know, felt rewarded, financially and otherwise, by coming to Harlow to exhibit. Most exhibits were for sale and the gallery was not supported by any outside funding but was completely independent. I found in time that sales averaged one third of the exhibits, and I also bought works for our collection. Roy Ray, who came to give a talk on the history of the St Ives art colony, commented, perceptive historian that he was; 'whatever else happens you will end up with a representative selection of St Ives art.' It is a collection ultimately destined for Harlow. My own painting received a tremendous stimulus from the art I was seeing and the artists I was meeting. Britt and I paid several visits to Honfleur in Normandy, the birthplace of impressionism, primarily for me to paint, and I exhibited in 'theme' exhibitions such as 'Townscapes' or 'Sea Images', shared an exhibition with printmaker Peter Wickham and gave myself a retrospective for the final exhibition.

Although I took no salary and the sales were substantial and increasing year by year, there was an annual loss. Tax laws, however, allowed losses from new ventures to be reclaimed from tax paid in recent years. With professionally prepared accounts I was able to do this, so the government subsidised the gallery. It was, you might say, poetic justice.

With the autumn of 1985, however, came its closure when the New Towns Commission took possession of the property. The display lighting and window panels were removed to our garden pavilion. It had been a great experience and I knew our partnership, in this case Britt and myself, had continued the development of Harlow. The local press had carried many items. The Tate Gallery had requested and received all my exhibition catalogues for their archive.

Our life was now to change. Things had happened in Sweden, and Britt's native country was to see more of us in the future.

XXVI

WE BUY A SWEDISH HOUSE AND TRAVEL

The family farm in Sweden was to be sold. Britt's nephew Bertil, or Böje as we called him, had taken it over after Britt's parents died, within a few months of each other, and had run it for several years. We had seen farming in this part of southern Sweden change. Labour intensive activities had gone, and animals had disappeared. The earth was too good for that. Wide fields of corn and barley, wheat or rye, rippled in waves under a clear blue sky and almost visibly grew. In spring the landscape was ablaze with brilliant yellow rape and the Swedish flag, a yellow cross on a blue background, had come to ground. A man and a machine could handle a huge area in the long light days. Böje loved it and worked all hours, repairing his machines with engineering skill, but he had taken over the farm coupled with a mortgage and in a period of high and increasing interest rates, when farm subsidies were lower than later, it became impossible to run. The land had now been bought by a nearby farmer, and the farm buildings would be separately sold.

It had been an ideal place for Böje and his attractive wife, Britt, to raise their two children and thanks to their generosity in letting us use the ground floor rooms where my Britt had lived, we had been able to spend our three week summer holiday there for many years, watching the children grow up, and bathing in the nearby Baltic. I had painted the wild flowers, the beach huts and the white churches. Now, after an intensely active three years running the gallery we would be able to spend more time in Britt's country, but we would need to find a new base.

At first we looked at summer houses along the coast; in the sandy pine woods behind the dunes, but before the wide farm fields began. In their sunny but relatively short summers the Swedes love to leave their urban dwellings and immerse themselves in nature, creating thousands of idylls—low timber buildings among the pines, leaving their surroundings as little disturbed as possible. These were beautiful but too primitive for us, lacking baths and, sometimes, inside toilets.

With another nephew's help, however, we eventually found something quite different. It was an atrium house in a sixties development on the outskirts of the small unspoilt seaside town where he lived. The extreme south-west tip of Sweden is a tiny peninsula separated by a canal. Its two

47   *On a sunny day in October 1985 I painted my last watercolour of the farm and we left for our new house*

48   *John Graham painting of the Temple Mount in Jerusalem seen across the valley from the hotel balcony*

small fishing villages of Skanör and Falsterbo had grown into small towns in their wealthy period during medieval times by exporting barrels of salted herring, an affordable food, to the Catholic populations of northern Germany and France during their fasting seasons. Following centuries, however, brought little development until 1904 when, with the growing popularity of sea bathing, a railway link was made and, in 1908, the first hotel was built in Falsterbo. They gained a reputation as the Swedish Riviera. Villas were built among the woods in Falsterbo including five during the period 1924 to 1936 by the Viennese pioneer modern architect, Josef Frank.

It was in the adjoining small town of Skanör that we found a development of atrium houses which had been built in 1968 by HSB, initials which I recalled in connection with admired designs in architectural magazines during student days. Nearly fifty years after its design it still offered a safe, private, peaceful and beautiful environment to a modern car-owning community and I was delighted to become the owner of an example of Swedish housing from its Golden Age.

Therefore, on a sunny day in October 1985 I painted my last watercolour of the farm and we accompanied our favourite furniture on a short journey to the new house. It had an open plan. One wall of windows opened onto a small private atrium, planted with vines, bamboo and honeysuckle by the previous owners who had been keen botanists. Inside there were plenty of plain, windowless walls which, once we had removed the traces of numerous indoor plants and had redecorated, provided ideal space for the St Ives paintings and prints which we were to bring with us in the Volvo the following summer.

The white and gold painted furniture from the farm had been made by a country carpenter in the classic Carl Johan style and its elegance of form and proportion fitted the house perfectly. Together, Britt and I created another interior which was a blend of Swedish and English elements, and even gave our relatives a strong reminder of the family farm.

With Britt's gift for hospitality we now became the focus for family get-togethers. It was an example of two cultures blending and enriching others as the partnership of Annia and Herodes had done in their time.

It was also, in the years that followed, a time for us to travel more extensively and for me to exhibit paintings locally. We had already visited Boston and New York in 1966 and had spent two weeks in Israel visiting Biblical sites directly after the Six Days' War when travel around that small country became suddenly much simpler than before, and much simpler than it has since become. Much of Sweden, however, was still to be discovered by us. It is a vast country, many times the size of Britain and its capital, Stockholm, is still only one third up its length. In fact, for southern Sweden the most convenient capital, just across the narrow waters, is Copenhagen.

49 The author's photograph of Swedish Architect Gunnar Asplund's Woodland Cemetery in Stockholm which was inspired by the beauty of Greek sites and justifies comparison with the Parthenon

Indeed Skåne was part of the Danish kingdom until fought for and obtained by the Swedes just over three hundred and fifty years ago. We had often been across to Copenhagen and enjoyed its art galleries and Tivoli.

Britt, however, like many Swedes, had never been north to Lappland, the land of the midnight sun, and one year we decided to devote three weeks to a trip. We drove north of Stockholm until we reached the great rivers gushing from the mountains on the Norwegian side which carried the felled trees from the great forests down to the sawmills in the towns on the coast. We found reindeer standing in nonchalant groups on the roads and then gliding off into the trees—their domain. We saw the villages where Sami lived, and passed through great marshy tracts where nobody lived at all. In our most northerly hotel rooms we heard lively conversation rising from the cafe in the court below at all hours of the night, while the sun sank below the western mountains without setting before rising again. In the pale, shadowless, light people were increasingly active. It was though they were trying to pack a year into these brief weeks. As we fell asleep they were still talking. Since then, the north of Sweden has meant something to us. It was no longer just the upper half of a long map which rarely got unfolded, and I was discovering the new country as Annia would have discovered Herodes' Greece. We also took friends on a visit to Norway. Oslo is not far from the Swedish border but Bergen, which was our goal, was a stiff drive over the mountains or, rather, through them, on a route with many tunnels. Nature here is on a grand scale, reducing the human being to insignificance. Bergen, when we reached it, was sporting fashionable umbrellas and we gathered that the rain, which continued throughout our visit, was to be made light of. From our Baedeker guide we learned that the mean annual rainfall is in fact extremely high, being over 78 inches, whereas Oslo has 25 inches! Grieg's villa at Trollhagen we found beautifully situated and the little writing house in the garden, where much of his creative work was done, proved to be another example of the tiny hide-out where artists prefer to work. The piano was up in the villa.

Our first visitor to the newly bought Swedish house had been John Brentnall from Tokyo where he taught in an English school. We had met him in the Harlow church when he was visiting his sister for the last time having decided he had found his 'natural' home in Japan. The visit to us in Skanör and then to Vienna was to be his final sortie outside Japan save for trips to the secret city of Peking. Hearing that Greta Garbo's ashes were to be brought from New York and re-interred in Gunnar Asplund's beautiful woodland cemetery in Stockholm he asked us to lay some roses there. After watching the ceremony on TV when a leading jazz saxophonist played a piece depicting her part of Stockholm we felt we could do this for our friend. The burial place had not, understandably, been publicised but we were led to find it easily. The crematorium, now a UNESCO World Heritage Site, is truly beautiful. Asplund was inspired, as he says, by the beauty of Greek sites and has created a partnership between architecture and landscape which justifies a comparison with the Parthenon in its grave dignity.

Although our exploration of Sweden would never have ended, there were some years when the urge to revisit Europe was irresistible, but this we managed to do 'en route' to Sweden. We drove to Prague just months after its 'velvet revolution' and experienced the 'joie de vivre'—dancing and jazz in the streets of that beautiful, undamaged city, while shops still displayed pyramids of cans for lack of other goods to sell. We continued on to visit the Bauhaus in a suburb of Dessan, known to me as a student through photographs but then inaccessible in East Germany. Now I could fully appreciate its ground-breaking design which, like the early Renaissance work, was breathtaking in its purity and freshness, but at the same time touchingly awkward in the details of radiators and window-opening gear which had yet to catch up with the modern aesthetic.

I wanted Britt to see the Spain that I had first experienced during the Franco years and planned a three week tour through 'old Spain'—not the tourist coastal fringe. A series of hotels was booked by telephone from Harlow and I still wonder at how extraordinarily lucky we were. Coming into the ancient walled city of Avila, with storks nesting in the high places, we found our hotel was right next to the cathedral! In Ronda the Hotel Reina Victoria had been Rainer Maria Rilke's favourite place for holidays! They even kept his bedroom, for which we were given the keys, furnished with editions of his books from which Britt read aloud some poems in German and their Spanish translations. I painted the powerfully dramatic landscapes the hotel windows overlooked. Cordoba, Toledo, Segovia, Salamanca and, of course, the Alhambra, were visited, although in the courtyards of that Moorish summer palace the tourists were now in full possession and the tranquillity I had once experienced was no longer to be had. This was the most exciting and demanding of all our travels, but although the car was fully loaded with items we were taking to Sweden, nothing was lost and the only effect was that the brakes soon needed re-lining after so much heavy mountain driving.

Sweden is a land of festivals: song festivals, food and folk festivals and jazz festivals—an interest which we shared with Böje. When the farm was no longer his responsibility he had some free time in the summer, which is normally the busiest time for farmers, and could join us. Not that he wouldn't have preferred to be working on the farm. This we knew without talking about it. One of the favourite jazz festivals for the three of us was in Kristianstad, the new town which King Kristian IV of Denmark had founded in 1614 as his capital for southern Sweden. The moat and walls which originally surrounded the town had been replaced by the planted Parisian-like boulevards and the rest had a simple plan not unlike Harlow, with two squares, small and large, linked by two shopping streets. From the outset it has been a garrison town. Where there were

50   *John Graham watercolour of Ronda landscape from Rilke's favourite hotel*

military men there were dances; ball gowns were needed. The tradition seemed to have lingered. There were several stylish dress shops in which Britt had more than a passing interest. Cafés were numerous and during the festival days the streets resounded to the sounds of New Orleans or Bebop, and on light summer evenings the main square filled with dancers presided over by a statue of King Kristian in his niche on a civic building.

I saw a 'new town' with a population smaller than Harlow's comfortably accommodating modern culture, while Harlow itself appeared to be languishing.

XXVII

HARLOW LANGUISHES. GIBBERD GALLERY OBTAINED.

Some of the town's key features which had given it character had disappeared. The college buildings at the opposite end to the Town Hall of the long upper pool in the Water Gardens had been moved out of the town centre. The sports centre, swimming pool and ski slope were scheduled to be demolished to provide sites for developer's housing which would finance a new 'wet and dry' leisure centre also on the new college site. The offices for the publishers, Longman, opposite the station, had been demolished and replaced by three buildings of mediocre design. The Master Planner would not have been pleased.

Most towns have a Civic Society but Harlow, as long as the Development Corporation, advised by Sir Frederick, controlled the town's overall design, had not appeared to need one. The need had now become obvious and a number of citizens got together and formed one. Stan Newens, former Member of Parliament and stalwart supporter of the Gibberd plan, had accepted chairmanship. I was elected vice chair and served for the first five years. We had failed to prevent the demolition of Longmans and its eventual replacement by three unworthy buildings but our voice was beginning to be listened to on planning matters at least, and before I resigned from frustration about the ineffectiveness of our architectural advice, I did have a role to play in a significant development.

The council, in partnership with the government's Commission for the New Towns, was seeking to redevelop the southern part of the town centre for additional shopping including very large commercial units. The vertical town hall which the council had never completed was to be replaced by a new, lower one; the Water Gardens would be moved slightly but reinstated, and the parking would be significantly increased. The major town space, the Civic Square, would disappear. This square had been part of the Gibberd Master Plan from the beginning and when the town was, virtually finished in 1980 and the Council and Development Corporation published *The Design of Harlow* to explain how the 'vision has become the reality of a mature and unique community' in the section on the Central Area the Civic Square is described as 'the principal entertainment and open air meeting place of the town …' 'for activities as diverse as symphony concerts and trade exhibitions … and exhibition gallery, clubrooms and restaurant.' With the disappearance of the Civic Square all this potential would be lost. The Civic Society had registered its opposition to the scheme, for which the Council were now seeking planning approval to proceed to detail design stage.

Sir Frederick's widow had occasionally called me a 'hopeless idealist' but I was enough of a realist to know that the Civic Society had absolutely no chance of stopping the scheme, but I was also aware that the council were uncomfortable with our objection. I therefore suggested to my council contacts that if, in addition to accommodating the Gibberd Collection which they were bound to do when the existing town hall was replaced, gallery space should be provided for changing exhibitions, and that if publicity and curatorial support be provided for these activities, perhaps the Civic Society would reconsider its position. The letter which came from them did include this offer, and Stan allowed me to take this part of the Civic Society's subsequent meeting. There was a full discussion. Nobody was happy with this major departure from the master plan but it was clear that if we withdrew our opposition there would be a significant cultural gain, for a programme of changing exhibitions would bring far more visitors to the gallery than a permanent exhibition could ever do. The meeting voted unanimously in favour of acceptance, with one exception—Lady Gibberd, who could never accept the commercial development which would flank the Water Gardens. It is a view the idealist in me absolutely respects.

Pat Gibberd and I had got to know each other several years previously when, as a result of the work I had done in running my gallery in the town centre, Michael Chase, at that time Director of Colchester Minories, proposed that I should join the Harlow Art Trust. I was delighted to do so. Our meetings, chaired by Pat, were at the Gibberd House—no longer displaying the large Burra watercolours and other paintings which had been auctioned off to pay legal expenses resulting from a family dispute regarding Sir Frederick's legacy. In winters it was sometimes cold, as the floor heating was expensive and the finances of running the house and garden were not then on a firm footing. Nor did the Art Trust have an income but depended on occasional sponsorships or grants. Some additions were, however, made to the collection and after considerable work an essential catalogue with superb colour photography by Graham Portlock was published in 2005 accompanied by a location map. Due to the initiative of Nick Bullions, then acting as our secretary, the Friends of Harlow Sculpture was also started, making what I had long regarded as an essential link between the sculpture and the citizens.

As the design of the new town hall or Civic Centre, began to be detailed, the Art Trust was consulted on certain aspects such as lift size, storage facilities, etc. Developers are not very forthcoming regarding the architects who work for them and I only recall once meeting the young man who appeared to be responsible for the design, but when it was complete we found that the Gallery Area at mezzanine level over the large entrance foyer was much larger than we could have anticipated and the character and quality of the building seemed to echo that of the 1951 Royal Festival Hall—something I would not have dared dream of in my most idealistic moments.

The town now had in its centre, a space of dignity and quality the equal of any London gallery and with a view out over the Water Gardens and parking to the open country as Sir Frederick would have liked. Whatever the commercial of financial pressures the future might hold; here was a place where Harlow's cultural life would continue its expansion.

The Gallery opened in 2004 and under three brilliant young women curators: Kelly Lean, Samantha Fox and Corrina Dunlea, presented a continuous series of high quality exhibitions. By 2012, however, in a period of national economic crisis the council was having to severely cut all but essential social services. The Gallery had been such a success and its growing prestige was doing much to create a different image of Harlow than the negative one the press and some who had never visited the town sometimes chose to project. The council, therefore, asked the Art Trust to take over its management hoping that we, as a charity, would be successful in obtaining funding. At that time, the Art Trust had recently sought and secured the name of 'Sculpture Town' for Harlow and were not without some doubts about running the gallery. I had not yet come across the Development Corporation's draft application to the Arts Council in 1954 for a grant for a group of artists studios and an exhibition gallery to be run by the Art Trust but even without this historical precedent it seemed natural to me that the Art Trust should do it as it concerned, just as the placing of sculpture throughout the town did, the health of its artistic and cultural life. This was the view which prevailed and in the spring of 2012 the Art Trust agreed to take over the management of the Gibberd Gallery.

In that summer an ambitious bid to the Arts Council and the Royal Opera House for funding was accepted. It seemed to me that things had now slotted into place; a wheel had come full circle. Both metaphors are appropriate.

While these changes were taking place on the Harlow scene and, during the summers we had been travelling widely in Sweden and elsewhere in Europe, the story of Annia Regilla and Herodes, which had been such a presence in our lives, had not been told beyond our friends. The real impetus to tell it more widely came from the most appropriate source—from the British School at Rome itself. I had not heard anything from them since we left Rome in 1954 and, due to our full programme in Harlow, Sweden and elsewhere, I had not kept in touch. But now, after nearly thirty years of mutual silence, came an invitation to take part in an exhibition of Rome Scholars' work at the Building Centre in London, prior to a tour. I welcomed the opportunity and, although I knew that there was still much to be learned about Annia and Herodes, I felt I could display my coloured measured drawing reconstruction of their building and outline their story. I was, however, due for a shock.

EPILOGUE

When I contacted the university to request the return of the measured drawing of the Annia Regilla building, which I had lent them, I was devastated to hear that it had been lost! Professor Cordingley had died in 1962 and the School of Architecture had moved into a new building. They sent me negatives of a colour photograph from which a large print was made for display with my photographs of the building as I found it and a brief telling of Annia and Herodes' story as I then knew it. It also showed my drawing of Banbury Castle Shopping Centre with the neo-classical facade of the former Corn Exchange which had been incorporated as one of the main entrances. This fitted in with the Classical tradition theme of the exhibition, although I was not in sympathy with the revival of Classical design for new building which was promoted by some of the introductory essays in the catalogue. Nor would Professor Cordingley have been. A third exhibit was the only 'free' painting in the show; the watercolour sketch of the Greek temples at Paestum which I must have been driven to make simply to record the beauty of their siting. Professor Cordingley's exhibit consisted of the large and beautifully sensitive measured drawings in pencil of the Mausoleum of Augustus which he had made when a Rome Scholar in 1923.

The exhibition opened on 28 November 1982 and I can quote from my journal entry for that day 'HRH Princess Alexandra really graced the evening with her presence. Completely informal, without introduction or speeches, she arrived and spent some three quarters of an hour looking round. We were just about the last persons she spoke to. Britt had caught her with a smile between the exhibition screens and she came round to see us. Learning we were from Harlow she recalled her hospital there …' Then, after a thoughtful enquiry about the draughty conditions which Britt might be feeling, she wished me to show her my work. So I led off to the appropriate screen and told her about the temple of Annia Regilla and the condition I found it in some thirty years before, when I measured it. She seemed genuinely interested—easy to talk to—tall and slender—fine-featured with a glint of humour in her eyes …'

At that time, which is, as I write, some thirty-two years ago, the personal details of Annia and Herodes in my description were taken from the guide to Rome by Georgina Masson, which Britt and I had used on our second visit to Rome in 1972. It was a suitably romantic story, I felt, to be telling to a princess. She seemed to be in no hurry and the three of us had a very pleasant time together!

Britt and I often thought about this first sharing of the story, and after busy years running the gallery and then travelling in Sweden and abroad, we now had a slower tempo. It seemed to us that the Civic Society would provide a sympathetic forum for the telling of it. So, in the sunny Spring of 2005 I set down our shared memories of the time in Rome, Vienna, Venice and Sicily and told the story of Annia and Herodes. The script was typed by the receptionist at the Tiverton Hotel while we were visiting our artist friend Peter Wickham.

Entitled 'From Harlow to Rome—at the British School 1953-4', the talk took place at Harlow Museum on 21 April 2005.

The unresolved question, the shadow cast by brother Bradua's accusation that brought Herodes to trial, remained unresolved. I knew there was research to be done before I could go into that. The evening, however, was not affected. A capacity audience found the talk exciting and there were many enthusiastic comments then and later.

That summer we went once more to Sweden and spent time with our relatives and friends, but it was to be Britt's last visit for, shortly after our return at the beginning of September and after a week in care, she died. I was able to stay with her and we were together all the time until our earthly parting, as we had been for over fifty-four years. Britt was courageous, and conscious, and almost her last words were; 'Now you will have time to read all those books …'—she might have added 'and to write one'.

After memorial services in Harlow and the following summer in Sweden I began to emerge to the realisation that life still held daily blessings and creativity never stops. One of the things which needed to be told more fully, I felt, was what we had learnt about Annia and Herodes. So, in the solitary hours which were now frequent, I began to read the books, even take some courses, to fill the gaps in my education (which had not been a Classical one). Initially, I thought I might be the first to be writing about Annia Regilla, but this was not the case. Research revealed the book published in 2007 with the lurid title *The Murder of Annia Regilla*. Surprised, I read it, expecting to find new evidence, facts, or witnesses to support the title, but I did not, only the author's conviction, from the opening pages, that there had been a murder, and that the murderer must have been Herodes, and that their inter-racial marriage must have been discordant. Fearing my reading might have been less than objective I got a writer friend to read and give an opinion. She confirmed mine. I now felt it doubly essential to write. One does not re-open a trial where the accused has been judged innocent, without fresh evidence, or give new interpretations without the possibility of a defending advocate challenging them.

In the research I got to know Annia and Herodes much better and discovered parallels between their lives and ours which I had not anticipated. Herodes has emerged as an emotional man, often at odds with his peers, a realist, ambitious, achieving remarkable projects, but also an idealist looking beyond his own times and loving the beauty which lies beyond the material; Annia Regilla, his chosen partner and support in all these activities, exercising a soothing influence, and creating a peaceful and beautiful home as a base for their generous hospitality and, in her service as a priestess, admired and even loved as reflecting a degree of divinity herself.

Like Herodes, I have now entered a period as a widower. He would not have let it become a period of Stoic passivity I know, and like him, I continue to visit my wife's country and spend time in the interiors we created together and the beauty we loved—beauty that transcends time.

51 Watercolour sketch of the siting of the sixth-century BC Greek Temple at Paestum

Britt Bäckström –
press notices 1949-1953

APPENDIX
Press Notices

Britt Bäckström, soloist tomorrow

Soloist in the Music Association's concert in the High School Hall tomorrow, Miss Britt Bäckström has earlier appeared at charity concerts etc., but now for the first time she is to perform with Trelleborg's Orchestra.

Miss Bäckström attracted deserved attention on her appearance at a fashion show in Trelleborg in the spring and lately as soloist with Malmö Symphony in their concert for schools, when she performed Scandinavian songs.

Miss Bäckström, who is the sister of opera singer Nils Bäckström has studied at Malmö Music Conservatory for singing teacher Connie Peters and has for her performances, received the most ample praise.

'Bgn' in *Arbetet* wrote as follows on 17 March 1950: 'If anyone should be mentioned, it must be Britt Bäckström. She has already acquired a quite developed coloratura technique, as she demonstrated in Mozart's "Hallelujah", and sang with both musicality and feeling.'

Symphony Concert by Trelleborg's Music Association

The concert included Haydn's 'London' Symphony, a cello soloist, Jan Karmazin from Czechoslovakia and 'in a special song section appeared for the first time as soloist in Trelleborg a young singer from the district—Miss Britt Bäckström. She showed she had an unusually rich and well managed soprano voice—even if she, from a purely technical aspect, is not yet ready. Her song artistry is exquisitely cultivated and she succeeded best perhaps with a little Romance by Carl Nielsen. The audience's applause for her was so prolonged that they forced her to sing an extra piece—Adele's coloratura aria from *Fledermaus* … Conductor and soloists were greeted with almost southern style ovations and bouquets—and the public were unanimous in their view—this was the best concert given here in Trelleborg for a very, very long time.' L.J.S.

'For yesterdays, they had the good fortune to find two outstanding soloists, who contributed greatly to making the concert as successful as it was … The evening's high point was however Britt Bäckström's songs with orchestra. Miss Bäckström has already on one occasion appeared in the town and sung herself into the hearts of the citizens of Trelleborg. With her shining and pure soprano voice and her thoroughly musical presentation she sang three Nordic songs just as they should be sung—simply and with warmth. Grieg's "Solveig's Song" suited her especially well: the little refrain with coloratura could have been written for just such a voice as hers …'

17 May 1950. Mannequin Parade in Trelleborg's Sports hall

'… the artistic highpoint was wonderfully beautiful singing by Britt Bäckström.'

'… the young singer Britt Bäckström deserves a special paragraph.

'Accompanied by Miss Elsa Borgquist she performed several enthusiastically received songs: "The Russian Nightingale Song" by Alabieff, "Die Forelle" by Schubert, and "Villanelle" by Bell Aqua. The young singer's light soprano delighted with its bell-like clarity and inspiration, and with apparent ease she executed difficult coloratura passages. The applause was spontaneous and sustained and at the end she received an ovation and flowers.'

Supper and Social Gathering in Malmö

'First, Miss Britt Bäckström gave a whole little concert programme including "Solveig's Song" from *Peer Gynt* by Grieg, Schubert's "Heidenroslein", Reger's "Marie Wiegenlied" and many others.

The young singer, who was on top vocal form, was accompanied by Miss Else Borgquist and reaped lively applause.'

27 January 1951. Concert for Schools in Malmö Theatre.

Britt sang 'Solveig's Song', Carl Nielsen's 'Aebleblomst' and Lange-Mullers 'Skin ud, du klare solskin'.

15 March 1951. Conservative Woman's Club Annual Meeting and Lecture.

'Miss Britt Bäckström, who received such ample praise for her song artistry on the two occasions she has hither to performed in Trelleborg, most recently at the Music Association's concert on Sunday, sings before and after the lecture, and those who hadn't the opportunity to hear her on Sunday, have now a possibility of having this experience.'

'… our own local singer Britt Bäckström…'

'… before and after the lecture Britt Bäckström made an excellent contribution to the evening's enjoyment. With her bell clear voice she sang a whole little concert programme, which despite the difficult acoustics, yet gave striking testimony to the fine coloratura talent we have in Britt Bäckström. She was rewarded with plentiful applause and flowers.'

24 April 1951 Malmö Women's Union

'Britt Bäckström (acc. Esla Borgquist) sang songs by Handel, Schubert, Alabieff, Strickland and others.'

Spring 1951 in Magareta Paviljongen. Malmö Pildamnsparken.

Solo songs by Britt Bäckström acc. by Inga Sarnstrom.

May 1951 Malmö Musikkonservatorium Student's Concert

'Britt Bäckström showed herself to have an even and well-schooled voice together with a forceful technique … in the coloratura numbers and the duet from *The Magic Flute*.'

29 October 1951 Musikafton in Trelleborg High School Concert Hall to end Lecture Society season

'Despite competition from other entertainment in town, the Lecture Society drew a large audience. But then it was Britt Bäckström who was responsible for the vocal part of the programme and she has already with her appearances won all hearts. It is not only the excellently sounding soprano voice one is captured by; the presentation itself is how if possible better than ever and must be the result of persistent study and deep personal feeling. One listens, deeply grateful, whether to Nordic "romanser" or songs from other lands and times. In the first part she performed three arias from *The Beggars' Opera*, an English opera from the 1700s, and one could only conclude that the baroque style particularly suits her clean and unsentimental way of singing. In the second part one hear a pair of Nordic songs of which Lange-Muller's "Lilla röde rönnebär" perhaps delighted most, and one heard it with pleasure again as an encore … Both singer and accompanist were thanked with well-earned applause and flowers.' B.N.

Musikafton

'A packed auditorium met Britt Bäckström and Gunner Rosenberg yesterday evening when they gave a soloists evening for the Lecture Society. Britt Bäckström sang first a group of songs from the 1700s and excellently brought out the melodies in these simple yet artful songs. But she succeeded even better with the Nordic "romanser" that made up the concert's second part. Such exquisite expression, such a pure and clear tone is rare. In these songs she seemed the complete artist.

'The public extracted a reprise of Lange Mullers "Lilla röde rönnebär". Need one say that the public was extremely grateful and that the soloists received many flowers …?' L.J.

2 Dec. 1951. Talk by Swedish MP Folke Kyling in Trelleborg's Stadshotell.

'Before and after the talks Miss Britt Bäckström sang to the acc. of Miss Elsa Borgquist several songs which were appreciated with lively applause and Mr Thidholm presented a charming bouquet of carnations to the "sympatiska singer".'

Music at Evening Service—Trelleborg's Church. April 1951. Preliminary Notice:

'Britt Bäckström is nowadays a very well known and highly appreciated singer in Trelleborg and we look forward with interest to her part of the music with songs by Bach, Handel and Mozart.'

'… In Trelleborg's church last Sunday, where a large audience gathered, there was yet another success for Britt Bäckström, who is well deserving of the appreciation show to her through the great interest which is expressed by the public. She is still studying, but already she has an enormous amount to give and her performance of her part of the programme became a devotional and memorable experience for her listeners …'

From the organ loft Britt Bäckström sang 'Bist Du bei Mir' by J S Bach, 'He shall feed his flock' by Handel, and Mozart's majestic 'Allelujah'.

'Everything ready for the premiere after a hectic week'

Trelleborg's Folkets Park Season opens on 1st May (1952) with singing by Britt and Nils Bäckström at 7 pm and 11pm (also see poster).

Reviews: 'BRITT & NILS BÄCKSTRÖM'—the singing brother-sister pair proved by their performances yesterday evening in Folkets Park a shining exception to the rule that no one is a prophet in his own country. We could only be at the 7 o'clock performance, but at that time there was scarcely an inch to spare between the packed listeners who filled the immense space in front of and around the open-air stage.

Both sang solos and duets from well-known operettas and other pieces. Nils Bäckström is already very well known and he sang as he usually does and reaped applause accordingly. Naturally, the greatest public interest was concentrated on young Britt Bäckström who was performing here for the first time. Despite the especially trying conditions for a singer—with the rawness of the cold evening air, she performed her part winningly and gave witness to her talent and skill. Her highly cultured voice rang out clear and pure and that she possesses unusual abilities as a coloratura singer was as clear as day.

She was met with admiration and warmth from the thousand-fold public. The singing brother-sister pair Bäckström's performance in the Folkets Park last night was something of a precious experience. At the piano Elsa Borgquist was responsible for the sensitive and supportive accompaniment. G.P.Q.

Bäckströms in the Folkets Park

Britt and Nils Bäckström yesterday gave the park's outdoor season a promising start in front of a crowded and delighted audience with a miniature concert.

The extremely attractive looking pair sang a duet from *The White Horse Inn*, but before that Miss Bäckström had delighted the listener with the purity of her bell-like voice in 'Chanson Espagnole' and 'Good Night' from *Victoria's Hussar*. Brother Nils performed a couple of his 'hits'—the 'Gondolier's Song' and the 'Grandfather's Song' from *Fagelhandlaren* and both as individuals and together the pair reaped lively applause."

Singing siblings drew record audience in Folkets Park

'Two siblings sit thoughtfully listening to the tape recorder playing the Mario Lanza programme from the other evening. He is dark and she is very blonde; actually they don't resemble each other in appearance, but are alike in having interest in music and being singers. May we present: opera singer Nils Bäckström and his singing younger sister Britt.

'Of the four Bäckström siblings only the young half have devoted themselves to singing but that ardently. Nisse Bäckström, his voice and roles we don't need to detail—the Skåne public knows him well by now.

'Sister Britt, on the other hand isn't as well known yet. With her twenty-two years she has had time to sing seriously for three. In contrast to her brother she has devoted herself to somewhat more serious things and sings for preference Nordic songs and Lieder. But that doesn't stop both of them sometimes joining in an operetta duet and with such a programme moreover, they succeeded in attracting a record audience to the Folkets Park in Trelleborg on the first of May.

'Young as she is Britt has known many difficulties. She has gone through a serious illness but it hasn't broken down her courage. She works perseveringly for her teacher her in Malmö, Connie Lundvall-Peters, and has tried her powers in a lot of performances at different functions. Her future plans are undecided as yet—there's still so much to learn, she says modestly, but the experts, amongst them brother Nils, consider that she really has a future before her with her singing.

Brother Nils has more definite future plans. He has already appeared in the first production of *Porgy and Bess* in Gothenburg and will have a major role in the Malmö production … when the season closes Malmö Stadtsteater goes on tour with *Kiss me Kate* and Nils is with them for half the summer—then on l August he begins at Oscar's Theatre in Stockholm when the big new musical *South Pacific* is to be given.'

25 November 1952. Charity matinee at 'Moulin Rouge'—Trelleborg.

Lizzy Stein and Britt Bäckström—'two charming singers both with deeply grounded popularity with Trelleborg's public. Britt Bäckström sang several songs from *Värmlänningarna* and a Spanish Song beautifully and with bell-like purity, and was greeted with lively applause.'

'Finally it was time for Britt Bäckström. In her usual cultivated way she sang three little songs from *Värmlänningarna* and a French chanson. She has a perfectly charming expression and a tone that sounds completely angelic. For every time one hears her she comes better and soon one must recognise her as being a complete artist. Her singing yesterday gave great hope of her future development. Her next concert, which is in the offing, is awaited with excitement.' L.J.

Spring 1953. Red Cross fashion show in Telleborg's Sportshall.

'The very large crowd were shown the most fabulous dresses and given exquisite music by a section of Trelleborg's Musiksällskap Orchestra and, last but not least, wonderful singing by Miss Britt Bäckström.

'Finally mention must be made of the flowers presented to our charming singer, Miss Bäckström, who gladdened the hearts of all the Trelleborgare with her excellent singing …'

Britt Bäckström to Vienna for singing studies. Autumn 1953.

The well known singer Britt Bäckström, daughter of Magistrate Johan Edvard Bäckström in Skegrie and sister of opera singer Nils Bäckström left yesterday for Vienna to study for eight months with the famous Austrian singing teacher Josepha Schramm, with whom Miss Bäckström studied for an equally long period last year. She began her singing studies abroad and then found her teacher through good friends in Vienna. Miss Bäckström has recently come home from a visit to England and plans to travel in spring to Italy for a couple of months' language study there.

Some other places Britt sang which did not received Press Notices:

- 24 February 1952. Malmö Sea Scouts Soiree in Limhamn. A musical entertainment by pupils from Malmö Conservatory of Music.
- 16 May 1952. Fashion Show in Trelleborg's Sportshall in aid of the Red Cross when Britt sang Grieg's 'Med en Primula Veris', the revue song from *Fledermaus* and Delibes 'Chanson

Espagnole'.

- At Burlovs Church. Sang a specially composed piece by Sven Welander on the occasion of the bishop's installation.

- At Gylle Church—solo at the funeral of Kantor Rosenberg.

- At Maglarp's Church—sang Max Reger's 'Maria Wiegenlied' at early morning Christmas Service.

- Concert in Trelleborg's church with organ.

- Bookday at Trelleborg's Stadshotell—several solos.

- Sang solos and duets with Nils Bäckström at annual dinner of Farmers' Association at the Savoy Hotel, Malmö. Also with Nils at another Malmö venue.

- For a Women's Association at the invitation of Gumnel Larsson.

- At Vellinge Gastis (Country Inn) after Christmas Dinners (2yrs) for Malmö judges and magistrates and their wives. (acc. By Elsa Borgquist)

- Sang at Höllviken's outdoor dance area

- Entertained with Bengt Wiksten at preview of Art Society Exhibition, Trelleborg.

- Several times soloist in the Christian Science Church in Malmö

ILLUSTRATIONS

1.	The Rising Sun Colliery, pioneer work of modern architecture by Prof. R A Cordingley.	2
2.	a) Professor Cordingley's axonometric drawing of the Markets of Trajan in Rome	4
	b) John Graham's cross-section drawing of the Markets of Trajan with dimensions	4
3.	a) The 1951 Festival of Britain	8
	b) in Stockholm 1952	8
4.	The entrance façade of the British School at Rome	12
5.	a-c) Annia Regilla's Cenotaph building as first seen in 1953	16
6.	Landscape near Veii. Watercolour by John Graham.	20
7.	The Ruprechtskirche in post-war Vienna. Etching by Wunderlich	24
8.	Marble carving of Herodes Atticus now in the Louvre	30
9.	The fig tree. An ink drawing by John Graham.	34
10.	Palazzo da' Mosto. Venice. Painting by John Graham.	36
11.	Photograph of the artist at work	36
12.	Townscape sequence in Venice 1954 photographed by the author	38
13.	a) Portrait of Britt Bäckström aboard the ferry to Chioggia	40
	b) The view from the ferry to Chioggia	40
14.	A Renaissance Composition of Roman buildings by John Graham in final year at Manchester University (1951)	42
15.	a-d) Rome as seen in 1953/4	44
16.	Doric temple at Paestum	50
17.	The ruins of Pompeii	50

18.	The interior of a sixth-century Greek Doric temple at Paestum	53
19.	In Sicily, Goats.	54
20.	Outside the house by the sea near Cefalù	54
21.	Cefalù Cathedral	56
22.	Apse mosaics from 1148	56
23.	Sicily. Author's photograph of the view from the ruins of Solunto.	58
24.	Turbulent Sicilian Sea. Ink and watercolour painting by John Graham.	59
25.	Athens. The Acropolis restored. A German archaeological drawing.	60
26.	Measured drawing restoration of Annia Regilla's Cenotaph by John Graham	80
27.	John Graham copy of a drawing by Antonio da Sangallo the Younger (1485-1546)	82
28.	First-century AD bronze statuette of a young woman. British Museum, London.	84
29.	An eighteenth-century engraving	87
30.	John Graham's painting of the interior and drawing of the exterior of Maglarp's Old Church in southern Sweden	90
31.	Two 'white' Skåne churches—Skegrie and Stora Hammar—paintings by John Graham.	92
32.	'Typical 1950s living room' in Felmongers, Harlow.	94
33.	Design drawings by John Graham for a proposed Harlow Arts Centre in 1955	98
34.	a-c) Harlow Market Square. Adams House and tile murals as originally designed by John Graham.	100
35.	Tower of Ward Hatch Church. Architect John Graham.	106
36.	Harlow's original town hall facing the future Civic Square	108
37.	Interior of Harlow's community sports centre	109
38.	Old Harlow redevelopment, The High Street shopping photographed on completion.	109
39.	Harvey Centre main mall drawing by John Graham to show materials	110
40.	Publisher Longman's headquarter offices seen from Harlow Station	110
41.	Harvey Centre's main mall at Christmas	112
42.	On sabbatical. John Graham paintings of Collioure.	118
43.	Renoir's garden, les Collettes.	118
44.	Britt beside Renoir's bronze of wood nymph 'Pomona'	120

45.	The headstones of Vincent and Theo Van Gogh	123
46.	Ibiza in 1949. Watercolour by John Graham, from the journal 'In Franco's Spain'.	124
47.	The family farm in Sweden; a final watercolour October 1985. Painting by John Graham.	132
48.	Jerusalem. The temple mount seen from the hotel balcony. Painting by John Graham.	132
49.	Author's photograph of Gunnar Asplund's Woodland Cemetery in Stockholm	134
50.	Ronda landscape seen from Rilke's favourite hotel. Watercolour by John Graham.	137
51.	Watercolour sketch of the sixth-century BC Greek temples at Paestum	145

BIBLIOGRAPHY

History and Architecture

Aurelius, Marcus, *Meditations*, J M Dent edition, London, 1906.

Birley, Anthony, Marcus Aurelius: A Biography, Batsford, London, 1987.

Cordingley, R A, 'Everyday Architecture', *Literary & Scientfic Society Transactions* Vol. XX 1938-40, Rochdale.

Everitt, Anthony, *Hadrian and the Triumph of Rome*, Random House, New York, 2009.

Eddy, Mary Baker, *Science & Health with Key to the Scriptures*, The First Church of Christ Scientist, Boston, USA, originally published 1875.

Graindor, Paul, *Un milliardaire antique: Herodes Atticus et sa famille,*. University of Egypt, Cairo, 1930.

Gibberd, Frederick, *Design in Town and Village: Pt 2 of Design of Residential Areas*, HMSO, London, 1953.

  Town Design, Architectural Press, London, 1953.

——— *Harlow: The Story of a New Town*, Ben Hyde Harvey, Len White with Others (publications for companies), 1980.

Hare, J C and St Clair Baddeley, *Sicily*, William Heinemann, London,1905.

Jellicoe, Geoffrey and Susan, *The Landscape of Man,* Thames & Hudson, London, 1975.

Kidder Smith, G E, *Sweden Builds*, Architectural Press, Bonniers, London, New York & Stockholm 1950.

Kidder Smith, G E, *Italy Builds*, Architectural Press, Bonniers, London, 1954.

Mumford, Lewis, *The Culture of Cities*, Secker & Warburg, London, 1942.

Masson, Georgina, *The Companion Guide to Rome*, Collins, London, second edition, 1967.

Neveux, Francois (trans. Curtis), *A Brief History of the Normans*, Robinson, London, 2008.

Perkins, Ward, and Jocelyn Toynbee, *The Shrine of St Peter and the Vatican Excavations*, Longmans, Green and Co., London, 1956.

Perkins, Ward and Axel Boethius, *Etruscan and Roman Architecture*, Penguin Books, London, 1970.

Pomeroy, Sarah B, *The Murder of Regilla*, Harvard University Press, Cambridge, MA, 2007.

Strong, Donald E, *The Classical World*, Paul Hamlyn, London, 1965.

Swedish Association of Architects, *Gunnar Asplund 1885-1940*, SAR, 1950.

Tunnard, Christopher, *Gardens in the Modern Landscape*, Architectural Press, London, 1948.

Wallace-Hadrill, Andrew, *The British School at Rome. One Hundred Years*, BSR, London, 2001.

Wright, Frank Lloyd, *A Biography*, Faber & Faber, London, 1945.

Art and Artists

Andrae, Christopher, *Winifred Nicholson*, Lund Humphries, Farnham, 2009.

Chauveau, Sophie; *La Passion Lippi*, Gallimard, Paris, 2004.

Clark, Kenneth, *Pierro della Francesca*, Phaidon Press, London, 1951.

Cross, Tom, *St Ives Artists 1939-1975*, Lutterworth Press, London, 1984.

Green, Lynne, *W Barns-Graham: A studio Life*, Lund Humphries, Farnham, 2001.

Jacobs, Michael, *Artist Colonies. The good and simple life in Europe and America*, Phaidon Press, Oxford, 1985.

Jones, Ruth; *Path of the Son – Monograph on Bryan Pearce*, Sheviock Gallery Publications, Cornwall, 1976.

Rilke, Rainer Maria, *Letters to a Young Poet*, W W Norton & Co. Ltd., London, 1954.

Whybrow, Marian, *Free Spirits. Jane & Tony O'Malley*, St Ives Printing & Publishing Co., St Ives, 2014.

Other Writings by John Graham

The Graham Collection, a 35-page full colour booklet to accompany the exhibition at the Gibberd Gallery, Harlow Council, 2006.

'Old Harlow Redevelopment', *Essex Journal* special issue Summer 1973, Phillimore, Chichester.

Designed in Harlow. The Work of Frederick Gibberd's Harlow Office, 1950-1983, a 10-page illustrated booklet to accompany the exhibition at the Gibberd Gallery, Harlow Council, 2008.

Sculpture in Harlow, contributions, with other trustees, to the volume published by The Harlow Art Trust, 2005.

Seven Poems from the Swedish, limited edition published by John Graham Fine Arts, Harlow, 1983.

Three Normandy townscape poems, limited edition published by John Graham Fine Arts, Harlow, 1984.

Allsorts. Six poems 1975-1979, limited edition published by John Graham Fine Arts, Harlow, 1985.

'In Franco's Spain'. An illustrated travel diary from 1949 (unpublished).